Rediscovering Cuba

Also by JORGE REYES
Guia Para Descubrir Tu Cuerpo
(Children's book in Spanish)

My words mean something and other poems

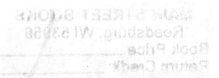

Rediscovering Cuba

A Personal Memoir

Jorge Reyes
Includes an interview with the author

Writers Club Press
San Jose   New York   Lincoln   Shanghai

Rediscovering Cuba
A Personal Memoir

All Rights Reserved © 2001 by JORGE REYES

Writers Club Press
an imprint of iUniverse, Inc.

For information address:
iUniverse, Inc.
5220 S. 16th St., Suite 200
Lincoln, NE 68512
www.iuniverse.com

ISBN: 0-595-19457-5

Printed in the United States of America

Praise for JORGE REYES'
REDISCOVERING CUBA: A PERSONAL MEMOIR

"Jorge Reyes takes us on his journey to Cuba and articulates the deepest, most achingly familiar feelings of his generation of young Cuban-Americans, those who grew up imagining the island as a sepia-toned place of their parents' fancy."
Liz Balmaseda, **The Miami Herald.**

"Jorge Reyes captures the spirit of every American who wants to learn more about his ancestry and from whence his family emigrated. One does not have to be Cuban to experience the joy and discovery of this family search. It is every man's story."
Ron Levitt, **President, Miami International Press Club**

"Jorge Reyes has written a special book, not only for those Cubans who knew the Cuba he describes with such special sensitivity, but for those-like him-who grew up far from their homeland and can only know it through family's histories that are often altered by time. Rediscovering Cuba awakens nostalgia, curiosity and fascination while effectively describing the realities of Cuba. The combination of Reyes' impression upon his return is precise, and wonderfully evocative. He allows us, his readers, to see a unique world, often surrealist and hilarious, in tragic moments. You won't be disappointed to rediscover Cuba with him, or visit it for the first time."
Frank Calderón, **CEO, Editorial Concepts, Inc**

Jorge Reyes' Rediscovering Cuba *is a humorous, poignant and philosophical treatise on the love of family and how that transcends the political differences that sometimes divides us. It left me yearning for memories of a Cuba I left over forty years ago, memories that are slowing growing dim with the passage of time and the deaths of the memory-keepers who make up the fabric of one's life. If you take away the specific references to Cuba, it is about any exile's journey home, their roots and the bittersweet realizations that the journey yields. Jorge Reyes' personal story touched me deeply and left me longing for the trip I've long wanted to make.*

      Maria Anderson, Commissioner, City of Coral Gables`

To the memory of my grandparents
Estanislao Figueras Alfaro
1908-1980

~~~

Isabel Luisa Alvarez Gonzalez
1913-1999

So much of you I crave to know.

ACKNOWLEDGEMENTS

Miles de gracias go to: Liz Balmaseda for her guidance, and Frank Calderón and Victor Delgado for their kind encouragement. The same goes for Clara Gomez, Irela "Lola" Ferrer (the 'IF' of many of my short stories), Hilda Marin, Sury Nieves, Lourdes Ponce, Carmen Lima, Zuzel Gomez, Cody Shiver, Raul Piñon, and my aunt Georgina de Almagro, who opened up after all these years.

I would like to especially thank the Miami Herald for publishing an excerpt of my work-in-progress in its Viewpoint Section and Gablers Magazine for the wonderful layout the editors did in their October, 2000 issue. Thank you all! Your encouragement was my motivation.

And, of course, this book would not have been possible without all the colorful and complex people I met in Cuba, family members and others. Your struggles, inspirations and fears are mine, too.

PROLOGUE

~ ~ ~

PART 1

~ ~ ~

PART 2

~ ~ ~

Let Cuba be reclaimed by this generation
(*Newspaper commentary*)

Descubriendo a Cuba
(*Newspaper commentary in Spanish*)

Interview with Jorge Reyes

All illustrations are courtesy of the author.

"This hour I tell things in confidence,
I might not tell everybody but I will tell you."

Walt Whitman, Leaves of Grass

PROLOGUE

I will never forget the look on my mother's face that day as she gripped the telephone receiver long after her sister had hung up. She was shocked. Paralyzed. Her hands were cold. Nothing could have prepared her for the news she had just received. Nothing; no evil portent; no black cat dashing out across from her on the street; no upside down tarot card foretelling an uncertain future.

When I touched her shoulders, she dropped the phone teary-eyed. I sat her down. What was wrong, I asked. Her sister Lisette had called from Cuba. The doctors had given my grandmother six months to live. Six months to live…

Did she want to go back? I asked. Not necessarily, she said, she was afraid. Did she feel she had to go back? I kept probing. This was different; she'd never forgive herself if her mother passed away without seeing her again one last time. I wiped her tears and asked her to call her sister Zuzel in Puerto Rico. I'd go with them to Cuba if they wanted. They needed it. I needed it.

Three months later, after visas, passports and 'special forms' were renewed, we, my aunt, 66, my mother, Grisell, 48, and I, 28, were on our way to Cuba: to the past. In the meantime, my mother kept calling Cuba every week. Was her mother better? Would she be alive before our arrival? In over twenty years, mother and daughter had not seen or written letters to each other, except once when they spoke for two minutes on the phone after my grandmother had agreed to be taken on a wheelbarrow to the nearest neighbor with a telephone. Every day that we waited seemed like another day that was wasted. And then it dawned on us how precious each of our lives is, how quick it comes to an end, and how powerful are the family ties that made us go back home—even as tourists in our native country.

My father came by the house to congratulate my mother on her decision. He had fond memories of Cuba, of her parents. There were tears in
his eyes. He wished us well. He wished her mom well. She had been like a
mother to him. Also for the first time ever since their divorce, his parents,
my grandparents Elvin and Bebo, came by to wish us a good trip. It was
not an easy decision to make, they agreed, since to most Cubans of the
older generation to return was to capitulate to the enemy: Fidel Castro.

We were going back. We were going back.

This is my story, no one else's; not the story of an exile community
though I, too, am part of that community. In these pages, I describe my
shock, dismay and ultimate reconciliation with Cuba. With some minor
exceptions, most of what you will read is exactly what I wrote while riding
on a bus, a taxi, or even a horse-drawn carriage. As for myself, reading this,
I'm perplexed by the many layers of memories I've been able to resurrect
from the deepest spring of my unconscious, a Proustian adventure into
self-analysis which would never have happened had I not gone to Cuba. I
haven't set out to rewrite history or analyze Cuba's present political climate
save by the few cursory observations I make. Far from it! From the beginning, I had something else in mind: to rediscover, relive and breathe the
air of that magical isle I hardly remembered, my native soil. As Vladimir
Nabokov said, 'speak, memory,' for who are we as people, as individuals if
we lose our gift of remembering, of retracing the steps whence we came.

Also, this is not a dispassionate memoir about Cuba or about the political, economic or social problems it faces. Unlike my ancestors, I don't
know what it means to be an adult uprooted from one's country and I
can't relate to what happened in 1959. I can only sympathize with those
who still yearn to die in their homeland; theirs is a lofty and legitimate
goal, the most magnanimous. What I can do is to maintain the current
discussion going on today about Cuba and that, in my case, began with a
family tragedy and went on to unravel into a personal dialogue with
myself.

To this day, I'm still trying to make sense of what I saw and felt and heard. It will take me years to understand what it means to be Cuban and what I felt returning to Cuba as a hyphenated person, a Cuban-American. I hope that, if anything, these musings will add to that rich history which is now over forty years in the making.

Many who have read the first edition of this book have asked me why I didn't write about Cuba's politics, or condemn its harsh realities. I have in subtle ways. Anyone who reads between the lines and lets him or herself be taken to the unique world I revisited, get to know the people I met and be introduced into my family, cannot but feel the pain the 1959 Cuban revolution has caused so many of us. Cuba *does* have a horribly repressive political system and there are documented testimonies about all of this. I encourage reading these narratives as I have done.[1]

In this new edition too, unlike the first, I have used many of the letters my mother wrote in the late 1960's and early 1970's to her future mother-in-law, my grandmother Elvin, who lived in the United States. I have printed them exactly the way they were meant to be read: as simple, as complex, as curt.

Regardless of how you feel, come with me and visit Cuba the way I did. It doesn't matter that you may not be Cuban. What I request, though, is an open mind and a healthy curiosity about the world.

Jorge Reyes
Miami, Florida 2002

---

[1] I am thinking of Armando Valladares' *Against All Hope*.

~ Part 1

CUBA

Boniato, June 17, 1976

Dear Granny:
I love you a lot... I received your letter... My dad is fine. Me

Had I not gone to Cuba, my dreams of Cuba would have been just that: letters with childish scribbles. Had I not gone to Cuba, the nasty hands of destiny and the merciless onslaught of time would have turned these letters into dust.

Boniato, June 23, 1971

Dear Granny, dear aunts:
I want to let you know that my mom already speaks to me about you. We are doing well and I'm doing even better writing you from my little crib. My dad is fine and loves me a lot. He talks a lot about you, granny, about how beautiful you are. I already try to get up, I move my fingers, smile, and often I want to sit by myself but they won't let me. When Elvita is born, I probably will walk. I think I'm going to be a big boy, a bit chunky and lily-white like my mom with the dark eyes and thick eyebrows of my dad. I gotta go now. Your grandson, Jorgito.

Had I not gone to Cuba, this world would have been a child's dream, letters with childish scribbles...letters yellowing in solitude.

Friday, July 17th was a typical summer day in Miami, hot and humid, with a cloudless sky dotted frequently by sparrows or airplanes. It was an excellent day to go to the beach and hang out with friends. South Beach's tourist season was at its peak; the clubs packed with the latest beats of trance or hip-hop; indeed, it was a glorious day. Except for my mother, aunt and I—we were going to Cuba. Of course, we had already said good-bye to family, friends and foe alike, this was, after all, not an ordinary trip. Since Cubans believe that Castro has personal knowledge of all who go back, we resigned ourselves for the worst—and yes, we were told to be careful, Cuban jails are horrible. Not to worry, my mother told everyone, this was a personal vacation, not motivated by politics. However, I wasn't at all reassured by her every time she would get in the car and drive to the church of Saint Jude, patron saint of the impossible, to light yet another candle – just in case. She prayed so much, usually at nights and under candlelight, that I memorized Saint Jude's prayer, "Come to my assistance in this great need that I may receive the consolation and help of heaven in all my necessities, tribulations, and sufferings…particularly about my trip to Cuba."

Since my mother had an appointment with her hair dresser that morning, she asked me to stay in the house to weigh the *'gusanos,'* the luggage, unmindful that I had done it about twenty times in two days, and to call about another half a dozen people to say good-bye.

"Castro está loco," she kept repeating. "You never know…"

The first phone call I got that morning was from my aunt Zuzel, who was going with us on the trip, inquiring about things she had already asked me many times the night before. Had the weight in the *gusano* increased? No, we hadn't added anything to it. Had the weight decreased? No, nothing had been taken out of it: not the shoes, the countless panties, shorts, shoes, medicines, dolls, yards of fabric, needles, yarns, band aids, you name it! At one point, at the last minute, she called and suggested we take a bottle of Ex Lax, just in case, and a bottle of water—Cuban water was substandard and full of parasites, she'd heard.

When my mother came home from the hairdresser, she didn't like her hairdo, so she washed it and ended up doing it herself. She then thought it would be a good idea to get a dog to guard the house for the week. Of course, in such short notice that was almost impossible, so we called on a neighbor whom we told of our trip and entrusted her with the house keys. The neighbor, oblivious of our plans, noticed that my mother had done something new to her hair, she couldn't tell exactly what, and complimented her new look, commenting that she had taken twenty years off of her. Vainly, my mother thanked her—that's exactly what she wanted to hear and she made her some Cuban coffee.

"I don't drink coffee," said the lady.

"Oh," my mother responded startled, "it won't matter, I'll drink it!"

Around noon, my aunt Zuzel and her daughter came to pick us up for the airport. At one point, making sure that no one was watching, my aunt cornered me and asked me cunningly, "Tell me the truth, did you weigh the *gusanos* correctly?"

I thought I was living among insane women. For the next twelve hours, to my irritation, my mother and my aunt spoke nonstop. In the airplane, I would close my eyes, tired already, and I could hear them bantering. I would open my eyes again, hoping to watch the sunset, and they were still at it. I couldn't believe it. They seemed to be an inexhaustible fountain of conversation. Not even Oprah Winfrey, Phil Donahue and Fidel Castro together would have spoken so much, for so long.

"Are we flying over Haiti yet?" My aunt asked at one point on the airplane.

"No," I said seeing a few lights in a horizon. "I don't think we have to fly over Haiti to get to Cuba."

"Oh yes, I thought I was going back to Puerto Rico," she said before breaking into a monologue about geography, Castro and the 'Haitian Peninsula.'

July 17th. What a day! This was a foreboding of what was to come.

~   ~   ~

From the airplane at night, Cuba's coastal line with its sparse lights seems separated, disjointed. Five minutes before the Mexicana airline landed, all of us on the plane looked down with pulsing heartbeats at the isle of our perpetual love. There were smirks on our faces. There were whispers, prayers, giggles. '*Yes,*' everyone seemed to say, '*this is Cuba, the Cuba of our memories, the Cuba of our dreams, the Cuba of our birth, the strangely seductive, always exotic land only 90-miles away from home.*'

"We're here!" said my aunt patting on our hands. We looked at each other. I think there was fear in our eyes.

At the Frank País International Airport in Holguín, we were treated like any other tourists, with polite reserved curiosity. Of course, we were far from being like any tourists—we were Cubans, or what was worse, Cuban-Americans. My mother told me to be polite lest a word out of line, an inappropriate statement, would get us in trouble with Cuban authorities. Nothing happened. My mother breathed a sigh of relief, probably thanking Saint Jude.

We boarded a jitney bound for the city of Santiago de Cuba, three hours away, about 11 o'clock at night. Our final destination: Boniato, a small town on the outskirts of the city.

None of us said much on the jitney. We were too excited. We were too scared. The roads were not very accessible as they were old with large potholes. Some '*campesinos,*' peasants, with their white cotton shirts, straw hats, and gurney sack slung over their shoulders, walked by the side of the road and would signal the jitney to stop. When the driver didn't stop, they hurled insults to us. The driver simply ignored them as he talked about his life (in Cuba, I noticed, people love to talk).

Besides us three, there were four other people in the jitney: two older sisters with a cantankerous girl who snoozed throughout the road trip on the downy softness of a doll and a middle age woman who seemed to be sleeping, in a trance, or passed out. Halfway to Santiago, we stopped at a tourist's hotel, the Sierra Maestra, to buy some refreshments. I went to stretch and heard the crickets, felt the early-dawn mist and the swooshing sound of plants and palm trees. Eerily, the hotel lights shone against a darkness made worse by the cool mist. My mother, trying to make my aunt relax, asked her to join us but she refused to get down from the jitney. She was afraid, and besides, she had a sore throat.

Our first contact with the unfamiliarity of this trip began a few hours later when trying to read in the dark the names of the streets in Santiago, my mother confessed to me that she didn't know where she was. She patted my aunt in the hands and asked, "Cuca, do you know where we are?" But my aunt, who left in 1968, was absorbed in her own retrospection. Undaunted, my mother asked the bus driver where we were.

"Up La Centrál," he said, "near El Hospital Provincial."

Seeing an avalanche of steps going up a ramp, my mother sprang on her seat, turned to me and said, "Your grandfather passed away in that hospital, I recognize that. Oh my God!" It had finally dawned on her that we were in Santiago.

As I was to see the next day and for the rest of my weeklong stay, much in Santiago has changed though in a strange way, like the rest of Cuba, much remains the same. It is true, many buildings and homes are in need of repairs. Some, fortunately, still stand and one can observe their former elegance under layers of decay and abandonment. But one has to look for these things, they take on lesser meaning under the struggle of daily living.

Boniato was minutes away. The jitney made a turn on a sharp bend and suddenly we saw our house fully lit at that early hour of dawn. We smiled reassuringly. The entire family was waiting for us.

And I was here, at long last.

~ ~ ~

My family's house is small with a charming entrance fenced in by intricately linked wrought iron grilles. Out by the stone facade of the house there's a large, *"Viva Fidel"* scrawl rumored to have been scribbled there by a member of the Committee for the Defense of the Revolution, the CDR's for short[2]. The house, built by my grandfather in 1951, is the house my mother grew up in, my parents married, where most of my five aunts married, where my grandfather died, and where my grandmother, 86, was still living.

All the years of absence dissolved as soon as we stepped down the jitney and saw the very familiar faces I'd often see in pictures: aunt Belkys, Mimi, Dalcis, Lisette, and my grandmother, Isabel Luisas Alvarez. They were older than I thought, more tired-seeming. Embraces, kisses, and tears ensued before we looked into each other's eyes and separation, that nasty word, was unknown in our lexicon. My aunt Dalcis looked at me and told me I was the spitting image of my father at my age.

In Cuba, family means just about anyone who claims to be blood related, however remote. The phrase 'immediate' as opposed to 'extended' family is unheard of. I got a taste of that by being introduced to first, second and third generation cousins, nephews, nieces, uncles and aunts none of whom we knew but who surprisingly knew who we were. Despite our differences, despite the political differences, if any, we were one, united after so long, if only for a short week.

I was transfixed, unable to move. The joy in Zuzel's face was indescribable. When the house was built, she'd helped her father design it.

My grandmother, propped up by pillows in bed, was wide-awake and talking to a neighbor, Nancy. When she heard the clamor, she called our names.

"*Mijito*, is it really you?" She asked joyfully, her face beaming. She'd been up all night waiting for us.

My mother hugged her, kissed her, cried. Belkys sat with them on a side of the bed and asked about my father. My mother showed them pictures of my brother, whom my grandmother had never met. She had a hard

---

[2] CDR's are local vigilante groups that purport to prevent anti revolutionary activities. Terror, distrust and personal backbiting are the ultimate result of these groups. Every true revolutionary is expected to participate in the CDR's, and those who do not are stigmatized, imprisoned and often fired from jobs.

time pronouncing his name, Ronny, named after none other than Ronald Reagan himself!

Later, when I was able to sit by myself, seeming to be lost in a distant land, I could hear the howling of a distant dog and the sudden sound of an owl desperately flitting above rooftops. Crickets chirped with a melody that only added further stress to my already lost sense of being. I was in a dream. While my family was talking, laughing, drinking beer, I didn't know what to do, or who to talk to. And to think that only twelve hours before I was in the safe surroundings of my world in Miami! And now, here I was, with people whose faces I could hardly remember, with voices that brought back a cascade of hazy images and memories. To quote Alejo Carpentier, "I felt myself yielding to an indefinable charm, a fabric of vague, remote memories and partly remembered longings."[3] The house of my first memories. The house of my mother's dreams. This was a dream, surely; a dream too real to roll around in bed, close one's eyes and pretend it was make-believe. The smell of coffee wafted in the air, not someone making coffee at that hour, but the smell of coffee of long ago, decades ago, when my grandmother used to percolate ground coffee beans from a woolen sock and wake up the entire household by its rich aroma. My eyes closed on me…yes, I was dreaming.

---

[3] Alejo Carpentier, The Lost Steps

Boniato, November 23, 1969

Dear Bebo:

Hoping that upon receiving this letter, all is well. I will tell you that we're in perfect health, economically not bad, and spiritually even better. I was waiting to write until today—Jorge's birthday—which is such a special day for all of us. Jorge and I are already engaged and my parents seem to like him. Everything went better than expected when he spoke to my dad. Our engagement is, alas, official. The only sad thing is that those whom he loves, you, his family, are not here to be part of this special moment. But don't despair, he's happy even if far from you. Tell Elvin that I will write her, too, soon, maybe next week. Her son, or shall I say, my fiancé, has put on some pounds, is a few inches taller and is very handsome.

Give my best to the rest of the family and my future sisters- in- law, Tatin, Elena.
Sincerely,
Grisell

PS: We received the stockings you sent us, they're pretty. Have a wonderful new year in New York—and for the future.

THE TOWN OF BONIATO

Saturday morning. My grandmother was in bed. She asked us to help her to a chair and about six people, mostly kids from the neighborhood, rushed to help her. I gave her a kiss. Dalcis had already bathed her from a tin pail in the kitchen and she smelled of cologne and powder talcum.

"I've wanted to see you so much again, Jorge," she said. She then turned to my mother and told her that she looked better than she'd imagined, not as '*engurruñada*,' a common slang for old, unlike her other sisters. (Actually, that word is closer to either being shriveled up or dried up.) She then closed her eyes, rested her head in her cupped hands and started to hum like a little girl. I think she was in pain. I snapped a picture of her. The picture has a transcendent aura about it and she looks in peace like a sleeping Madonna with a tired countenance.

I walked out to the patio and I gasped. Everything seemed so deserted. Everything looked so sad. Beds of weeds grew wildly and untended everywhere. No ducks, roosters, pigs, goats or any of the farm animals my grandparents kept roamed about. My mother's dollhouse had been torn down throughout the years and the wood used for '*leña*,' kindling. The trellis on which grapes and wisteria vine grew had rotted, fallen to the ground and disintegrated among weeds and the ravenous hunger of termites. The patio also looked smaller, not as large as I thought it was, just a patch of land on which not a tree grew. There used to be a mango and a huge avocado tree under which I used to stand for minutes at a time and look up at the clouds and at the birds and at a sky that seemed limitless and shifting from under my feet. Now that my memory was returning, I also remembered a large palm tree whose coconuts dropped with frequency—to my terrible shock and pain.

My heart sank. Once a happy boy made this patio his own private heaven, played with all the farm animals, climbed the many trees, played hide-and-seek and rescued sick birds from the branches of trees to raise them to health. Once a happy girl, my mother, played with her dolls in her dollhouse caring little for the world except the world of her own private garden. Their laughter and their joy, their simple, meaningless echoes of yesteryears, dispersed in a wind that abruptly swept all my memories aside. I walked back to a grimy and unkempt kitchen. The tiles on the kitchen cabinet were cracked or loosened; the walls were covered with soot; the high colonial ceiling wrapped with a fine sheen of cobwebs. The bathroom had no running water, and as I was to see later, if I wanted a warm shower, I had to first heat the water in the patio in a tin pail over a fire. The same went for the toilet.

My cousins, Alain and Alex, each a year apart, dropped by and asked me if I wanted to walk around Boniato like in the old days. Today, they had taken the day off from work so I took my backpack and off we went!

Boniato is a small town. Lore has it that it was built atop an old Indian cemetery and it is still very much a town of '*guajiros,*' poor and illiterate peasants, and farmland. It is rich in vegetation with a constant smell of brush fire. From El Puerto de Boniato, a popular tourist attraction on the mountains, one sees Boniato and the city of Santiago clearly, like a freshly-painted watercolor. The port is silent, conducive for meditation. The benches are strewn with dead leaves that fall from tall, rugged trees. The leaves rustle under your feet with a strange, sober sound. Dozens of royal palm trees, tall and elegant, sway in a coffee-infused wind. On one side, there are '*bohios,*' thatch-roof homes, clinging out from under acacia brushes.

Boniato had a river behind Francisco's farm, close to our house. I used to come here in the afternoons after school and skinny dip with friends. Most of the time, I went to the river by myself. I loved the silence, the introspection. Old rugged trees rustled weightily with the breeze and their roots cleaved out from under the ground giving them a false sense of imbalance. Often an occasional guinea pig was caught in the thick bushes and their frantic squeals could be heard from miles away. Time and nature, however, have all but changed the river's current and what used to be a mighty river is now a brook on whose marshy sands cows graze.

"Jorge," said Alex, "do you remember the skeletons you had?"

I chuckled.

"How can I forget?" I asked.

A cousin of mine who was a medical student had two skeletons. For many years, she kept the bones dissembled in a plastic bag and one day, wanting to get rid of her bizarre keepsakes, she asked me if I wanted them. She didn't have to ask me twice because I was already hauling home the bag of bones! Swearing him into secrecy, Alex and I spread the bones on a bed and with the aid of my encyclopedia, I started to assemble the bones: a femur here, a rib cage there. Hours later, the skeletons were assembled but they still looked too naked and sad, so I dressed them with old petti-coats and spread oleanders on them. I named one Fefita and pinned a nametag to the dress. Well, I thought it was funny, but not for long. My grandmother walked in on us and seeing us, she rolled her eyes, started to scream with an, "*Hay Dios Mio! Que horror! Hay!!!!!*" and conjured the many curses that would befall us throughout our lifetime. Alarmed, my aunt Mimi came to her rescue and when she saw what we had done, she gasped and stumbled against the wall before fainting. It didn't take long before my mother, bat in hand, rushed in on us, but she proved to be the anti-hero in this comedy of errors and she, too, fainted. Soon, I had a room full of fainting women as I, holding the skull of Fefita, could do nothing but recite, "*that skull had a tongue in it, and could sing once...*[4]"as Hamlet did holding the skull of Yoruck.

"It was funny," I said. "The whole room turned into a funeral parlor."

We walked through a little bridge past beautiful homes encased in a wild profusion of wild trees, ivies and bougainvilleas. Little shacks with no

---

[4] Hamlet, Act V, I, 48-88

running water, kitchens, or bathrooms except for latrines, ran alongside these homes. In front of a home, a boy named Albertico was being bathed from a tin pail by his mother and when I turned on the camcorder, the mother, excited, started to call her other kids to, please, come out and take a bath with Albertico. In Miami, this would be frowned upon.

"Albertico," I yelled, "aren't you embarrassed to be making dirty movies?"

Along with his mother, siblings and grandparents, Albertico began to laugh uproariously.

My old school, Antonio Roberts, is an old Victorian structure with long corridors and French windows turned elementary school after 1959. It still has the feel of a church. For the first three years of my school life, I stood in line in front of the school, held my fisted hands to my heart, and promised to be like Ché: *"Pioneers for the revolution, we will be like Ché!"* We'd then listen to current events: *"A U.S. invasion is imminent!" "Jimmy Carter is a Wimp!"* and on special occasions, we'd perform a play. I once was chosen for a leading role. Unfortunately, at the last minute I forgot my lines, started to cry and the old teacher had to play the lead. She glued on a moustache, dressed in pants and told the beautiful girl, Leonela, how much she loved her!

Before the revolution in 1959, my mother attended the same school and she hated it—she never got along with the nuns, they were too stern, she said. Right next to the school a bar has been built and the owner is none other that a former teacher of my mother's, one of the nuns. That afternoon, salsa music was playing loudly from a jukebox. Ice-cold beer, pork rinds, and black and beans were sold at a counter—all of it, of course, sold with dollars, not pesos.

Amen!

~   ~   ~

Without a map to guide us, the next day, Alain took us in his car to El Zaino, farmland deep within winding roads, past countless little brooks and hills about fifteen minutes from Boniato. From El Zaino, one can cross to El Cobre and see the shrine of La Virgen de la Caridad del Cobre, Cuba's patron saint. At one point, the roads became inaccessible and Alain asked us to continue on our own with my aunt Lisette as guide. He'd wait for us on that spot, he said, as a stray cow ambled next to him and eyed him suspiciously.

At El Zaino, my grandfather, Estanislao Figueras, bought his first house and a 12- acre farm before moving to the present home in Boniato. The house there, a small, wood-framed shack with dirt floors still stands—incredibly so—where an old black woman named Melba lives with her daughter. They own pigs, chicken, a goat and two cows. When my aunt Lisette introduced herself to her, a dog chased her out and the old woman didn't even bother to quiet it.

From the outside, Lisette gazed hungrily at the house as if she, too, were trying to preserve something of her past.

"It's still there…" she said.

"What is?" I asked.

She pointed to an old tree in front of the house. "The ceiba tree, look at it!"

Lisette went on to tell me an anecdote of how, in the 1940's, swinging so high from the same tree that she lost her balance, she fell down through the palm-thatched roof dropping on the living room and slashing her cheeks with a flint stone on the dirt floor. She pointed to the thin scar on her cheeks that she still bears proudly like a birth sign.

We kept walking.

"Those were difficult days," she said. "Your grandfather's milk was often confiscated. Whenever that happened—which was often—we'd go hungry." She stopped. "That was during Machado's dictatorship. I got horrible memories from those days. Your mother had not been born yet." She inhaled deeply; the air was cool, crispy, unpolluted. "Whatever you

may hear about Cuba in Miami, remember, we've tried to do what's right
for our country. Do you understand?"

I shook my head.

"Do you understand?" She repeated and I shook my head again, qui-
etly. "But poverty has it own charm, its own sweetness."

"How so?" I asked, intrigued.

"You see, since we were so poor your grandmother never had a pair of
shoes to wear…"

"Oh?"

"Yet, she never went without one…you see, she was so crafty that she
came up with this way of painting her feet with white shoe polish to pretend she had shoes."

Great, the Martha Stewart of Cuba! I laughed.

"She did this every time the occasion called for it, like when her mother
Pepilla visited us on the weekends."

"And Pepilla never knew?" I asked with a chuckle.

"I don't remember, I honestly don't."

I looked about me, thinking how my grandfather had walked these
same dirt roads and would never have guessed that I, a stranger to him
now, would feel the need to retrace his steps. And yet, strangely, I felt so
out of place and alienated from this world. Unlike him, I've never had any
major problems in my life; I've never struggled as hard as he did; I've never
gone hungry.

Lisette continued. "Your grandmother was always coming up with ways
to make money to help your grandfather meet the household expenses.
Once, she came up with the idea to sell kindling wood in packets of twelve
wrapped with red ribbons."

"Ingenious," I said.

"Yes, very; unfortunately, competitors drove her out business," she
laughed and lit a cigarette. "I wish I had her spirit."

Little by little, memories of my grandmother's craftiness were coming
back to me. "I remember she sold milk in the black market and when she

wasn't arguing with my grandfather, she made cheese from curdled milk to sell as well," I said. "I'm amazed she was never caught."

Lisette opened her eyes. "She wouldn't have been sent to prison, she had the head of the CDR under her belt, remember, she never sold him undiluted milk!"

We laughed. My grandparents always watered the milk they sold their customers.

We got to my grandfather's ranch before dusk. The ranch is an impenetrable jungle, the outhouse long gone, with pieces of rotten beams strewn here and there. What would my grandfather have said if he saw his ranch in ruins, reverting back to the forces of nature? Death must be a blessing to some, surely.

"A river would flood this area during the rainy season," my aunt pointed to the brown, humid soil.

"Your grandfather almost drowned here once. Luckily, his overseer Furungo saw him and saved him. Now look at it, there's no river." I asked my aunt who this Furungo was, I'd never heard of him. "Oh, we passed his house, he's still living, he must be over a hundred years old."

The river has dried, how true, like everything inside of me that craves to be Cuban. No, on second thought, the river hasn't dried, it's '*fango,*' mud, with a remnant, a spark of its former self breathing under the merciless Boniato sun. The river has not dried, not completely anyway; it's concealed under its own shadow, ready to burst once again, one day, whenever that may happen to be.

At that moment, it began to rain and gnats clung to our sweaty skins. We walked back to the side of the road where Alain was waiting for us in his car with his new paramour, the lost cow.

As usual, when we got back to Boniato, more people were waiting to see us, like my third grade classmates. They asked me if I remembered them and I shook my head. I asked about my friend Enriquito. Oh, someone said, he left to the United States, where he now lives in Pennsylvania.

My grandmother asked us where we'd gone. When we told her, she smiled with a questioning look in her eyes. Why, she seemed to ask, were we going to El Zaino? What were we expecting to find? She grinned.

"He (my grandfather) still visits me in dreams," she said. "He talks to me about everything."

"Does he *abuela*?" I asked.

She shook her head convinced of the reality of her dreams.

My grandmother was not very talkative, that day or for the rest of our stay. In fact, as I noticed, she said very little. Silence, perhaps, was her means of sanity. As I observed for the rest of my stay, she would look at you from far away, trying to make out certain recognizable physical traits in your face. She was old, though she had aged gracefully. She had a mop of white ashen hair and deep lines around her eyes. I will tell you something in secret: she didn't always have gray hair because she usually dyed it purple by letting soaked carbon paper dry on her hair.

My mother, always in the mood for a good talk, tried to talk to her about my grandfather.

"Look over there," said my grandmother pointing to a small drawer with no door next to her bed. "Those are your father's shoes, remember them?" And she went to sleep. After that, I knew she didn't want to talk about El Zaino, or anything related to it. Therefore, if I wanted to know more about my family history, I would have to go to other people for bits of information and towards that end, I'd harp on anyone who'd known my grandparents way back then when they were young and the future seemed all the brighter.

Boniato, November 28, 1970

Dear Elvin:

Always hoping that each letter I send finds you with joy and prosperity. We are doing well. Your grandson already kicks in my stomach. His little feet seem to be made from stone. Can you believe I'm already six months pregnant? We are expecting the baby sometime in March 6th or 7th. The first time Jorge felt him kick, his eyes watered with joy.

Elvin, I received the postcard you sent me for my birthday. I also received one from my sister-mother, Zuzel. How are the girls? Tatin and Elena…and how about Yoyita…she must be a pretty young girl by now!

Your son Jorge is fine. Everyday he's a better man. He is very loving and loves my mom. She loves him as well as the son she never had. He says that we are his family now: my mom, my dad, my sisters. One must love those who love us back.

Tell Tatin and Elena that I enjoyed the wedding present they sent me. I will write them some other time.

Jorge and I spent a few days with your sister Cuca and Maria Emilia in Havana. They are wonderful women, very loving, very sweet, in contrast to this world of ours we are living in.

Your grandson Jorgito has lots of beautiful things ready for his birth into the world. Above all, everything is new, not handy-me-downs. My sister from Puerto Rico sent me yarns of fabrics to make him baby clothes and my mom is already hard at work making them. I also have a baby crib. Everything is ready.

I know I keep calling him. But don't worry, if he is a boy, which we are hoping, his name is Jorge already. If a girl, we will name her Zuzel Mercedes, a

combination of my sister's first name and your middle name. Do you like it?
Jorge wants a girl in a year or two, but I don't know, things in Cuba don't seem
to be getting any better. Things are bad, very bad.

Anyway, as always, send my love to the girls and Bebo, 'Ramanaqui'. Tell him
not to get mad at me because I haven't written him lately. I will soon, I promise.

Grisell

MY FAMILY

My mother kept asking herself why my grandmother hadn't said anything to anyone about her illness. If she'd said something sooner, maybe, the doctors could have saved her. Unnerved by the silence that surrounded my grandmother's terminal disease, I asked my mother what was wrong with her.

She shook her head. "It's lung cancer," she said with a sigh, "and it's spread to the rest of her body. I never thought this would happen, that she would die." She breathed deeply, closed her eyes. "I have so many beautiful memories of my parents."

"Where were you born?" I asked.

"At El Zaino. In that house you saw. I was born there."

"What a long road it's been," I mused philosophically.

"Very long…very long indeed…longer than you can imagine. You see, son, each road is joined by another just like it before, which is joined before by another and another until the beginning of time, as far back as you can imagine." She smiled. "Yes, it's been a long road…. very long…unfortunately, it's all swept aside unless you reclaim it over and over again…unless you relive it…"

I asked her to tell me my family's story, a part of it, whatever she could remember. She sat down with me and began to tell me the little she knew, the little she could remember. She was able to go back to the times my grandfather was a kid in Marimón, one of the poorest neighborhoods in Santiago, near the renown Santa Ifigenia Cemetery, where the remains of the Cuban leader José Martí are buried.

Most of the homes in Marimón are built of corrugated tin sheets clamped together and held by wooden beams. In Marimón, there's a pungent smell of urine and excrement and burning fuel. There are horse-drawn carriages with tired, bony mules clamping up hilly boulevards. Coal ovens made of concrete blocks burn at all hours of the day, effusing the air with the whooshing sound of steam water, or the agreeable smell of burning roast pork, or any of the many delicious smells of Cuban food. Anywhere you look, you can see people walking or waiting for the next carriage or bus.

Children, mostly black, play marbles and laugh joyfully out by the porch of their homes, careless of their immediate surroundings, probably the same way my grandfather played a little less than a century ago.

My mother and I went to Marimón in an old beat-up car, although we never found the house my grandfather lived in because no one remembered where it was. But it didn't matter. Each of these homes was the exact replica of the other, joined together in their poverty, wedded into one another by their sameness. Each or all could have been his home.

My grandfather comes from a very humble and poor family. When he was seven years old, his only pair of shoes was worn out and he refused to go back to school. When the school's director inquired about his whereabouts, his sister Esperanza told the teacher that he'd died of typhus. After that, he went to work for an American chocolate factory called 'Cocolique' where he was promoted to supervisor years later. It was at this time, in the 1920's, that he met a teenager, my grandmother, who was 16, from a borough in Santiago known as *El Reparto Sueño* and they fell in love. Her mother did not want him for a son-in-law because of his poverty. So, they eloped and went to live with his mother, Mamá Vieja, Old Mother, where they lived until they married, three months later. In the meantime, he found a small job in a dairy farm called 'Guaninicú' and learned all about administering a farm, his job for the rest of his life. Sometime after, they bought a small acre of land and named it El Zaino, their future home. The first home they built at El Zaino burned down shortly after Zuzel's birth. My grandmother, in her rare outbursts of religious faith, lit a candle to La Virgen and before she knew what was happening, the few things they owned went up in flames.

My grandfather's family, like all of my family from either side, is originally from a town in Spain called Figueras, whose last name he bears. From the pictures I saw, his father was a rugged, ruddy-faced Spaniard.

Family lore has it that once in a lover's quarrel, his neck was hatched and he was left for dead at the city's dump. While everyone took him for dead, three days later, guess what: there was a resurrection. He got up on his own two feet, went back home, and cured himself with herbs and leaves. After that, he was nicknamed Machetaso, or Hatched-Man. My grandmother's father, José Alvarez, met a similar twisted fate. He was run over by a locomotive he didn't hear because he was deaf (apparently, he was blind as well), and, not to be outdone, her mother, my great-grandmother, Pepilla, died of a heart attack after arguing with a flock of pigeons that was pecking at her food. Yes, I admit, my ancestors were an odd group.

While visiting the cemetery, we visited the family gravesite. About twenty family members are buried there. One of them is a Estanislao Figueras, who died in 1908 with no date of birth. The same goes for his wife, Catalina, who died in 1917, with no date of birth either. My grandfather, another Estanislao Figueras, died in 1981, but the slab on the crypt does not list him. But it doesn't matter. He's not buried in some distant land, or in a lonely plot in Miami surrounded by tawdry shopping centers, like his doting sister Esperanza. He's here, and that's all that matters.

My great grandparents, Pepilla and Machetaso, were not the only eccentrics in the family because the Figueras girls, my aunts, had a knack for inheriting their 'odd' ways, especially Mimi. Mimi was a mischievous but quiet little girl: even at a young age, she was fond of drinking, not alcohol, of course, but a strange cocktail she made of earth and ground coffee. One of these things was a strange mix of earth and ground coffee that she loved to drink. No one knew anything about this until she got very sick. Taken to a hospital, doctors could not determine what was wrong with her. At a loss, giving up, the doctors sent her home to die— none of the prescriptions they gave her seemed to work. However, days went by and Mimi would not succumb to death. My grandmother was baffled and scared: her little girl seemed to have a supernatural ability to come back from what seemed to be an assured death. As a last attempt effort to save her, my grandmother took Mimi to another clinic in

Santiago. By then the doctors were even more perplexed, and one doctor made an educated guess and concluded that she was suffering from typhus (there seemed to be an outbreak of typhus in Santiago in those days).

"Typhus? Is that some sort of plague, like the black plague?" My grandmother asked.

"She's going to die," the doctor reassured her.

My grandmother, sobbing, took the weak girl in her arms and sat outside the clinic on a bench. Luckily, a nurse who had just finished her shift saw her crying and asked her what the problem was.

"My daughter's cursed," my grandmother said, "she's got the black plague and she's cursed with the evil eye, she won't die."

The nurse looked at the girl and asked her to wait; there could be a solution. She came back with a palliative and asked if she could give it to her.

"Sure," my grandmother said. "What do I have to lose?"

Mimi, breathless, unconscious, was made to drink a formula and soon she started to defecate a strange mixture of coffee beans, earth and parasites. No one had ever seeing anything like it. Not even the doctor. My grandmother gave thanks to all her saints, and Mimi was saved.

It wasn't long, however, before Mimi was back to her mischievous ways. My grandfather had an old cow named Rosilla. Because the cow was old and had become a family pet, it was allowed to rummage through my grandfather's farm unhampered. Slaughtering Rosilla the Cow, as she became known, was not a choice. One day, however, my grandfather began to notice that the cow's milk production was decreasing rapidly. Surely, the cow was old but not that old, and thinking that a neighbor was milking the cow for his own use, he resolved to investigate. One morning at the crack of dawn, he hid under some bushes near the spot the cow slept. Shortly, as he had expected, he saw a shadow moving among the trees: the culprit was coming. He got up, steadied the rusted machete and springing forward who does he sees but Mimi under the cow holding one of the udders to her mouth! Years later, laughing and reminiscing in Miami, my grandfather's brother, Chago, now over ninety years old, told me the story and said, "That's it! Rosilla the Cow was Mimi's mother, she raised her like her own daughter!"

Boniato, August 1973
Dear Elvin:
Of Jorgito, beautiful. He loves to eat and it shows! Sometimes we give him six meals a day. He is the spitting image of his father. He likes to talk, or tries to talk, and he seems to understand so much and know us all. He acts older than he is and sleeps well. Jorge, as always, wants another baby, a girl, he says... but I don't know Elvin, I'm only 21! I guess I can wait 5 or 6 more years or wait until we can leave this country. If things work as well as they have, we may even be able to move to a house of our own.

Tell Tatin that Jorgito has a picture of her and takes it everywhere he goes. He seems to be in love with his auntie already! The other day my mom and I were ironing his clothes and when he saw the shirt you sent him, he took it from us and hid for a few minutes with it. We tried to coax him to return it but he refused saying his beautiful granny had sent it to him. Can you believe this kid? Already stubborn and pig-headed like the rest of the family.

Your son is doing well. I don't approve of his friends, but what can I do? Overall, he is a good man and he misses all of you a lot. It's been now five years (since you left), hasn't it? Time flies. Have you changed a lot? Your son is now an adult. When you left, he had just turned 18.

Anyway, I got to go back to my chores. I will write sometime, soon.
Grisell.

MY GRANDPARENTS, BOOKS AND IMMORTALITY

When I was in the fourth grade, I decided to be my grandfather's teacher. Every day after school, I would come home and teach him what I had learned that day (it didn't matter that at times I hadn't understood the lessons). Soon my aunt Belkys, a teacher, brought me a small blackboard and soon, blackboard propped against the wall in the bedroom, history book in hand and a stick to threaten him if he gave me wrong answers, I became the youngest teacher alive. There was just one subject I was forbidden to teach: Fidel and communism. One lesson in particular stands out. I wanted to prove that Yugoslavia was somewhere near Havana while he tried to impress on me that it wasn't anywhere near the Caribbean! I didn't give up and he finally agreed whispering cunningly behind my back, "But it isn't anywhere near Havana." The poor Galileo was confronted with a modern version of the Inquisition.

I taught him for about a year and as time went on, I think that he actually looked forward to these daily rituals in knowledge according to his eight-year-old grandson. When he got too sick to continue, my afternoon classes were cancelled. He was rapidly loosing lucidity, and he was turning somewhat senile, or as we Cubans call it, '*chocho.*' After that, he became a sort of loner who found himself more at ease feeding or pretending to talk with his ducks and roosters than with people. Once, thinking he was going to milk his cows at El Zaino, he swooped under the clothesline and walked all around Boniato with a pair of panties caught in his hat.

I remember my grandmother more fondly, perhaps because I knew her longer. She was a great storyteller, unlike my grandfather, who was a joker. Had she lived in another place and time, she probably would have been either a writer or a very eccentric bohemian. Encouraging me to do anything that my heart desired as long as I did not get involved in politics, she once asked me to rewrite the Old Testament, which I tried and failed but not without a good laugh, a pat on the head and a "Good try!"

The stories she told me were odd, if not gruesome. One of these stories was of Delgadina, a nice, proper Spanish girl from the upper crust of Cuban society. (I can't believe I'm able to remember this!) Delgadina's mother was very beautiful and her dad was good but very stern. They owned a ranch, carriages and had many slaves. Delgadina's mother tended a beautiful garden with rare, exotic flowers of the most brilliant colors and fruits of the most delectable taste. Once, Delgadina's mother forbid her to eat a grape from the grapevine—the only grapevine in Cuba that would beget grapes for the next thousand years. But being mischievous, one night, Delgadina plucked a grape from the vine and ate it. She liked it so much that she ate another one, and another one, until she ate all the grapes. The next day, her mother discovered that her grapes were missing. Immediately everyone knew who had done the mischief because that same day, Delgadina woke up with a horrible bellyache, and her face was blue. Her father, to punish her, did one awful thing: he buried her alive. Three days later, however, a beautiful tree of long black shiny hair grew in the backyard, and to the family's discontent, they discovered that it was Delgadina's black hair. They trimmed the tree of hair but three days later, it grew back. The entire family was very distressed because now not only did the tree grow the most beautiful locks of black hair anyone had ever seen in Cuba but the tree sang as well, *"Delgadina, Delgadina, I've been buried for the grapes I've eaten."* The family went crazy over this because their cruelty drew the ire of the Cuban gods and soon, the curse of the gods was upon them, and the family lost their ranch, their carriages and their many slaves. With time, the beautiful garden with the rare, exotic flowers of the most brilliant color and fruits of the most delectable taste dried, and there were no more flowers to see or fruits to eat, except the sad songs of the tree of hair that could be heard at all hours of the day.

My grandmother and I were avid readers. In time, I decided to write and unlike my attempt to re-write the Old Testament, to my amazement, words flowed from my pen easily. The character I liked most was of Maria Eugenia, a prostitute, who lived on the second floor of a tenement project. Unfortunately, she was always jailed and in defiance let her hair grow to such lengths that she was never able to walk again. (It never occurred to me that she could have her hair trimmed.) I loved to paint and sketch, too, and I filled hundreds of pages of notebooks with my scribbles. I would then flip the pages of the notebooks and narrate to myself what I thought the sketches meant. If toilet paper was given for that month from the "ration book," I would steal these rolls from my grandmother's kitchen cabinet, unroll them, draw in them and then roll them back and pretend they were film reels whose images I would project onto some screen. My imagination ran wild!

I knew so much of the world because I read so much. Of course, there were many things I didn't understand. I would read about crime, passion, communism, and it seemed that the world was brimming with excitement at all hours of the day and I wondered why I wasn't allowed to get first-hand experience of that great world out there. In fact, I was a very sheltered boy. I never played with the neighbor's kids. My friends were very few. I didn't even like school. It was too political! Too histrionic! I had to follow rules of personal grooming, which I hated. If I let my hair grow, the director reminded me to trim it, I didn't want to look like a girl—did I? If I would tell my mother, she would fume and rant about everything that was wrong with Cuba. Eventually, though, she would have my hair trimmed and I would have my locks of hair swept away under a dirty broom. I hated the old barber. When I got too belligerent for him, my grandparents found a barber from Santiago who would come to our house every month to trim my hair. That man was even older and every time he raised the scissors to nip at my hair, his hands would tremble. I was flabbergasted. Didn't anyone see he was a danger to me? What if he took a nip at one of my ears? I, of course, couldn't take this. So, I came up with a plan: what if I frightened him by pretending to be possessed by the devil and when he least expected it, I'd start to channel and speak in tongues? This, I felt, would do the trick. So, on the appointed day, just when he was about to trim my hair, just below a whisper, I began to groan with a husky voice, *Ofimatedelacutarera!! Oh Mephistopheles, prince of darkness, come and take this weary boy!* But nothing happened. He wouldn't react. He wouldn't even question me. I couldn't understand it. Who wouldn't be afraid of a kid who boasted to channel with the dead? After a while, demoralized, I found out the problem: the old barber was deaf. Undaunted, I decided to come up with a better idea, something that would embarrass him beyond redemption. My plan took a month to concoct...and it was very simple. The next time he came, after he finished butchering my hair, as he turned around, I pinned a donkey's tail to the back of his pants. How simple! How swift! When he felt a small tug to his pant, I gave him the brightest, widest smile and he smiled back, unsuspecting. A month went by and on his appointed day, he was a no-show. One more week went by and nothing. My hair was getting longer. Worried, my grandparents wrote him a note inquiring about his health and whereabouts—he was old, they figured, he could have died. Days later, he sent them a note of apology, thanking them for their kindness, but unlike the gracious people that they were, I was a brat, a monster, a changeling, and a few other expletives. He went on to explain the mockery he endured the previous month by people in the streets who brayed at him when they saw the cute, colorful donkey's tail with tassels pinned to his back. And I had done it! After all, I was a monster! I spoke with the devil himself! My grandparents threw a fit. I didn't care. According to someone named Niccolo Machiavelli or *The Prince*, I couldn't remember who, any act that furthered one's goals was legitimate and hence correct. I never saw the old barber again, but I was taken to the neighbor's barber, now a woman after the previous one had died of a heart attack.

Both my grandparents supported my love affair with books, my whole family, really. If anyone offered them a gift for their sweet, beloved grandkid, they told them that unless it was a book, not to bother. Ironically, I never had a large book collection. Quicker than I could finish a book, they disappeared, and there was a good reason for that. For a while, I didn't know who was doing this, or why. Since Belkys had a nice book collection she forbid me to read, I blamed her. By blaming her, I thought, I had a right to search through her book collection, casually inspect her own books, and maybe—just maybe—'borrow' a few for myself. She defended herself like a tigress, calling me a brat, a tattle tale and a liar. But no one believed her, or no one chose to believe her. Poor Belkys, she wasn't liked by the family.

One day, however, dozens of torn pages of my books began to appear in the patio crunched up into little balls and with a repugnant smell. It wasn't long before I figured out what was going on: my family was using the pages of my books as toilet paper. I couldn't complain, of course, since I was just as guilty as they were for stealing the scarce toilet papers they received once a month, if at all.

With my grandfather's death, I began to ask myself deeply-troubling questions about life in general and about our place in the universe. Unlike my grandmother, who was healthy and strong, he was a sickly man, always seeming to be at the hospital with something or other, "*achaques,*" and when that happened, we thought that this would be his end. But bounce back he did, a resurrection of sorts, and eventually we thought that he would never die, he was one of the immortals. As he always liked to remind us, the secret to longevity was a strong belief in saints, especially Saint Lazarus, his favorite. After all, saints demand little from their mortal sons and daughters, maybe a candy, a pastry, or their favorite, a cigar, if one was available—in those days of austerity, cigars were like gold nuggets. My grandmother blamed his ailments on stress forgetting that he suffered from frequent pneumonia and diabetes, prompting him one day to yell at her, "Evil woman, you're gonna kill me with your mental counseling!"

"He's just a crying baby," she'd say. "Just look at him, he cries over anything." Which was true, my grandfather loved to cry, for any reason, like two of sisters, Isabel and Esperanza, who were professional weepers.

But no one in life is immortal…my world was about to crash soon!

One night, he started to complain about a horrible pain on one side of his body, a slithering-like pain that went up his legs, up his spine and up his chest. He asked my grandmother to call Mimi's husband, Guajiro, to give him a ride to the hospital. My grandmother, out of habit, woke the household with a bang of pots and pans.

"He's stressed out, again," she said. "Somebody take him to the hospital!"

We helped him to get dressed, miraculously found a cigar which we put in his pocket and with much fanfare saw him go as if he were going on a vacation. Even his mutt Rabito, lapping at his feet and licking at his boots, howled, wishing him a speedy return.

"Hey, anybody, Mimi, Grisell, Jorgito, please don't forget Saint Lazarus," he screamed from inside the car as Guajiro drove away. "Don't forget to smoke a cigar to Lazarito under my name." Apparently, he didn't remember I was forbidden to smoke. That was the last time I ever saw him. It was a few minutes past midnight.

Early one morning, a week later, my father drove up in a taxi to tell us to rush to the hospital, the doctors were not counting on my grandfather living past noon. This took us all by surprise—wasn't he immortal? We borrowed cars from friends and neighbors and headed to Santiago. My grandmother didn't say much. I don't think she even cried. She was sitting in the backseat of the car and I was sitting in the front. When news of his death reached us, she patted me in the head and asked Dalcis to take me home.

That day in Boniato, I felt an irreplaceable void unlike any I had ever experienced. As I was to feel many times later in my life, death is always felt by the void that's left behind, by the silence, by the unnerving disquietude you feel. It just seemed, and it still does, so unfair that a life of struggle or a life of riches, amounted, in the end, to the same. My grandfather had worked so hard all his life, endured so many hardships—and for what? If life had this for him, I thought, what redemption could exist for any of us, for me? Even if spirits existed, as I kept hearing, why was it that no one wanted to die? My grandfather, I know, was petrified of death and unlike most Cubans, he actually hid himself under the bed sheets if anyone spoke about having seen an apparition.

Remembering that I had to feed Rabito, with a bowl of milk in hand, I started to look for him, 'Rabito, Rabito, here, boy, *heeereeee, boy*!' Personally, I didn't like the little mutt. As a puppy, someone had tried to poison him but my family had saved his life by forcing him to drink hot liver oil. After that, he was never the same dog. He was a filthy thing and when he lay down to rest an army of ticks would surround him. His eyes were strange and lidded, his bark unlike the bark of other dogs. He also had this strange mocking-like smile, like a hyena. Whenever there was a full moon, he would leap in the air and start to chase shadows, prompting us to believe that Rabito was a special dog and his erratic behavior nothing less than him chasing away evil spirits. And yet, no matter how many times I called him that day, he would not come. I looked for him everywhere, by the river, by the bridge, by the park, and nothing. In the ensuing days, even my mother searched for him. But no one heard from Rabito again. He disappeared the same day my grandfather died.

My grandfather was buried in the family plot the next day. The grave had already been emptied, just in case someone might need it. Cubans exhume the bodies of their loved ones after three years in order to make room for another. The bones are cleaned, washed and powdered before they are placed in little niches alongside the wall inside the grave.

Weeks went by and my mind was filled with horrible ideas about death that no one could help me answer. My grandmother was no help since she was in mourning, and my aunts did what she asked them to do. Silence reigned in our house. To break the monotony of our household, I started to say that I could see spirits and my grandfather's shadow. I don't know if anyone believed me because I was never punished.

"How does a ghost look like?" One of my aunts asked. I don't remember which one.

"Well," I said looking at the ceiling, "ghosts are brown."

"Brown?"

"Yes, very brown, browner than the brown of chocolates."

"Are ghosts black, then?"

"Possibly," I said, beginning to feel uncomfortable by this line of questioning. "From what I see, all ghosts are brown."

My family was probably proud that I had inherited some psychic abilities from a line of bastard children on my grandfather's side, or like their beloved pet dog Rabito. Most likely, though, I was still influenced by Odysseus' journey to Hades, where ghosts are said to be disemboweled shadows. Why was I allowed to read so much? To this day, I can't come up with an answer.

Finally, tired of the silence that surrounded me, the hush that always followed one of my 'smart ass' questions, I asked my mother why people died. She, depressed and withdrawn after my grandfather's death, was sitting on a block of concrete watching mindlessly the string of puny watermelons my grandmother grew at that time. She looked at me strangely but not surprised and made up a story about how it is necessary for someone to die to make room for another, a quota system of sorts. So, logically, I asked, my grandfather had died so that someone could be born? She shook her head, uncomfortably. But, it's so unfair, I probed her, what if my grandfather didn't want to die this month, I know he didn't! Would that other person about to be born have to wait for his decision? My mother was at a loss for words. She didn't know what to answer except that her look expressed either amusement or great concern. But the stern look softened and she cracked a smile.

"Sure," she said, "you will never die, you are immortal."

~   ~   ~

The ghost of Ramiro, Esperanza's son, still haunts our house. He doesn't want to leave the earth, not even after all these years. On many a nights, his whispers can be heard and his shadow can be seen under candlelight. Back in 1952, he came to live with my family after his mother threw him out of the house—they never got along. She was so poor that whatever little money she earned, he'd steal. When they argued, which was constantly, in spite, he'd take all her living room furniture and put it out on the streets. Ramiro's dad had passed away days before he was born, so, as logic went, everyone assumed that my grandfather could fulfill that role and Ramiro was sent to live with my family in Boniato to help around the farm.

One day, he felt light-headed, like butterflies flying inside my head, he said. My grandmother gave him *manzanillo* tea and aspirins, but the headache intensified. He was prayed over to no avail, and he was taken to a physician who diagnosed him with leukemia. Typical of Cubans, this was kept secret from him—not easy in a house with six girls. Belkys, his childhood archenemy, was warned that if she said anything to him she'd be tied to a tree for a week unfed. During this time, Ramiro fell in love with a Jeep a neighbor was selling, and knowing that his days were counted, my family negotiated to have the Jeep loaned to them for a few days until he died. You should have seen Ramiro's face that day, one of my aunts told me, he was very happy. Unfortunately, he never had time to ride the Jeep for that same day he took to bed and died.

Years went by, decades, and to this day, my family swears that the smell of dead flowers from his funeral still regales the air. That may keep his memory alive—that and his picture in my grandmother's bedroom. He looks at you defiantly, with dark, brooding eyes. A ghost, surely, that will always haunt my family by banging on walls and by the eternal smell of flowers from fifty years ago. When his mother Esperanza died in Miami forty-eight years later, old, senile, and bitter by resentment, she was buried with an old black-and-white picture of Ramiro in her hands.

THE CITY OF SANTIAGO

"Smile for the camera," I say to my grandmother.

She smiles weakly and shrugs her shoulders.

"I'm too old to smile," she says. "Besides, I'm not getting married."

"Marriage?" I ask, taken aback by her strange statement. "Well, it doesn't matter, even if you don't marry, I think you're still cute," I say, camcorder in hand.

We've been in Cuba for three days and this is the first time I am having a conversation with my grandmother, however strange.

"OK, I will smile and I will marry," she says.

"Who are you marrying?"

She looks at the camera, thinks. "I'm going to marry the devil."

"The devil?" I ask again surprised by her response.

"He's a cool chap, he just has a bad reputation."

"Yeah, but why *him*?"

She looks at the camera and, again, shrugs her shoulders. She puckers her lips and says, "You're a bad boy."

She turns around in bed, she wants to go back to her dreams. I turn off the camcorder and help her fall asleep.

~ ~ ~

I was asked by my mother to accompany her to see my grandfather's oldest living sister, Isabel—one of the weepers—86, and her husband, Iginio, 98, and so we did. Yes, they are that old!

Isabel and Iginio are living history. Not too long ago, a newspaper from Santiago reported that they were the longest-and-oldest living married couple in the entire city. Isabel is physically strong though her mind runs astray. She's deaf and usually responds to your questions with typical Isabel answers: whatever comes to her mind. Her great-great-granddaughter told me that Isabel thinks she gave birth to a baby girl whom she later abandoned at the shrine of El Cobre, and once, highly distressed over this, Isabel called her many expletives, and ended her diatribe by asking her to refrain from speaking to her again, *puta*, thank you so much.

Iginio is more lucid of mind. He has owlish eyes under bottleneck glasses, as if the eyes of Minerva were looking right at you. He spoke about my grandmother as if she were a young woman, going so far as to say that she *is* very pretty, one of the prettiest girls in El Sueño. Afterwards, the affable Iginio gave me a guided tour of a picture gallery in his bedroom.

"That's me," he said pointing at an old daguerreotype. "And that's my mother and brother, who fought in the war of '95 (1895), and that's someone I don't remember (Ramiro)," he paused. "I think he died."

He turned to the picture with wandering eyes, turned around, and walked away, leaving me in his bedroom.

Iginio is old Cuba, forever indestructible.

Their three daughters told us that they sympathized with the government, but that family is family, and despite our political differences, they welcomed us as one of their own. One of their sons, a distant cousin, works for one of Cuba's arts & cultural departments and often travels outside of Cuba. He told me that he was surprised that I was so pleasant to talk to considering that most of his experiences with Cubans from Miami during many cultural exchange programs have been less than friendly. In particular, he mentioned Rosita Fornes, a Cuban singer living in Cuba who was forced to cancel her shows in Miami after Cuban exiles threatened to burn down the place she was slated to perform in. I think the restaurant went bankrupt thereafter. I know, I told him. Yet, I went on to tell him, even though arts and politics should never mix, this has never been true of Cuba, or of any 'revolutionary' system, whether from the left or the right. Curiously, he listened to me but said nothing. I think he was afraid of another confrontation.

Isabel and Iginio sat side by side as I took their pictures. They stared at the lens of the camera, hopeful and yet withdrawn. For a brief second, a frightened smile appeared on Iginio's lip and as the flash went off, I knew I had preserved a part of history, their only companion now. When we left, he asked me to give Belica, my grandmother's nickname, a kiss for him.

"She's Machetaso's daughter, Little Machetica. What a gal she is!"

We left their home and a friend of my cousin's gave us a tour of Santiago in his car. Oh boy, was it hot in Santiago that day! The car, obviously, had no A/C, and there were six people in the crammed car! The *Santiagueros* walking about looked tired, weary, like the homes that were about to fall on them. Vultures flew in the sky and danced to the whipping wind, dipping down in a sudden thrust and charging up again as if afraid to remain on the earth for long. (Vultures, so typical a bird in Santiago, have always revolted me after my mother once told me that they loved to feast on dead people. Of course, it wasn't long after that when, flint stone in hand, I inspected the sky for any signs of vultures carrying away the dead under their sharp talons. Usually, when an animal died in Francisco's farm, flocks of black vultures, their six feet feathered wings stretched wide, would swoop down from the sky after circling for hours, and sit atop the carcass to devour it.)

Santiago is full of rising and winding streets. Modern roads give way to old cobblestone streets within the same block. Santiago is the oldest and second most important city in Cuba, founded in 1514 by Diego Velazquez, whose house in El Parque de Cespedes has been restored after a fire burned one of its wings and is now a museum. Long separated from the rest of the island, Santiago has developed a unique history that can be observed almost at once. The people of Santiago have always been rebellious and mischievous, a trademark acknowledged with pride and honor. According to a reference book I read at the *Elvira Cape Archives*, over 29 generals have been born in Santiago. Beautiful natural sceneries are everywhere, like the Gran Piedra Mountains that stretch across the land down to the sea. The climate at the Gran Piedra is very cool, strangely at odds with the hot weather in the city. The highest mountain looms thirteen thousand feet above the city. Important coffee-producing farms, now in ruins, are named after French conquerors: *Henriette, Marseillaise, and Mont Roux*. *La Enramadas* is the center of commerce, where many stores still bear their original name, *El Encanto, Le Louvre*. The old Sears, now called *Cubalse*, is still a department store. *Padre Pico* is an interesting street built on steps, one hundred to be exact. The hospital I was born in, *Los Angeles*, is still there, next to which there is a huge billboard of Antonio Maceo with the inscription, '*La Patria Ante de Todo*,' The homeland before everything.

The *Vista Alegre* neighborhood is, or was, the posh neighborhood of Santiago. Certain sections in Vista Alegre reminded me of the homes in Coral Gables in Miami with its many Mediterranean-style mansions. Yet, unlike the Gables, many of these residences are boarded up, dilapidated, or have been turned into boarding rooms. I was so taken by one Victorian mansion in particular with wide, open porticos, moss-covered walls and a garden fountain, that I walked in to ask permission to take a picture. I knocked at the door and no one responded. I knocked harder and the door wobbled in slightly. Intrigued, I pushed it in slowly and the warm sunlight trickled to a cold empty living room with no walls, sagged ceilings and portraits that had fallen to the wood floors. Thick cobwebs shone with the sunlight and briefly, just briefly, life seemed to bounce back from an eternal dark emptiness with echoes, just echoes, and merry cheers. I wanted to walk in, unearth the thousands of secrets in each whisper, in each song, know what the past had to say to me, the present. The mansion was in ruins and I walked back.

We stopped the car to meander around the narrow, quaint streets of Santiago. Browsing through a selection of Marxist dogma at a bookstore, a woman approached me to ask me for a dollar. I gave her the dollar and as she ran she almost tripped over a table, afraid to be arrested. My cousin told me that with the dollar I had giving her, she could buy food for the entire family.

The presence of undercover cops, informants, in Santiago was everywhere. How can anyone live like this? I asked myself. How can an entire country fall under this most detestable form of scrutiny? Am I at fault? Are my parents and grandparents and the people living in Miami at fault? Or is the truth a bit more complex? Perhaps the truth is sadder, more tragic, because we're all at fault. Perhaps we're all at fault because there is no single victim in this war of ideals and love of country. We're all responsible; *I* and what I represent for leaving Cuba as if we were going to a summer cottage abroad; *they*, here, for being too complacent, too easily taken by a man. Why have we all taken the easy way out and wait…. wait…wait for who knows what! Wait for death to liberate them! But as someone once said to me, I'm too naïve, who knows what horrible truth lies behind this veil of sorrow that's called Cuba.

Tired, I saw a convenience store and asked my cousin and his friend, the guide, to come in with me. However, without our knowing, the guide was stopped at the door by an undercover agent who had been following us. The guide was asked a battery of questions. Where did he work? What was he doing? Where was he going? Not once did the undercover agent look at me, as if I was of no consequence, a shadow not worth bothering with. The guide told me not to worry, to go in and buy food while he waited outside. My fear, my sense of unfairness, my desire to protest meant nothing to a blind and depersonalized representative of the Cuban Revolution.

"OK, fine," I said frustrated. "I'll get you guys a Coke or something."

As I pushed the door, on the glass window, I caught a glimpse of Ché's face from a glossy black-and-white poster with red letters across the street. His head is tilted to the side and it's difficult to say if his eyes are full of anger or benevolence. For a second, I felt disoriented, but then I realized that what I had seen was a mirage, an illusion, and I walked inside, to a store catered to my bourgeois appetites.

ON OUR OWN IN SANTIAGO

My mother told me that in her dreams she often walked the streets of Santiago. We were in bed, late at night, and she was talking to herself, knowing that I was listening, knowing that she was not dreaming. A small air conditioner in my cousin's bedroom roared like an ancient beast about to come out of its lair. The lights from the San Antonio church, where my parents married, the only building fully lit at that hour, shone through the threadbare curtains.

"For twenty years in my dreams I kept seeing the same parks, the same trees, the same schools, the same people. They never aged, ever. I'd walk like a god on water, freely, supernaturally, and I'd see your father, wave at him, and I'd continue walking up Enramadas, Quinteros, Cuabitas until I'd get to Boniato and see my mother again, just as I left her, purple hair and all. I never told anyone about my dreams. No one."

Yes, mother, I know. Thinking of Cuba is like eating a guava pastry. Hot and melting in your mouth, dripping in your hands as you take a bite, arousing the senses to ecstasy. Thinking of Cuba is like roasting a pig under guava leaves, tamarinds and *mojo* dressing, lemony and zesty to the taste. Thinking of Cuba is walking into history, into the past. Thinking of Cuba is a smell that never loses its aroma, a lifelong dream that never ceases to enrapture, embolden, and it dies with you.

Suddenly she turned around in bed and said: "You know, we should walk around Santiago by ourselves! Just us. Let's see how much I remember."

~   ~   ~

Apparently my mother remembered very little of Santiago because wherever she took me, we got lost. Finally, giving up, she started to ask people for directions to a certain address where someone named Edith lived and then she asked how far her address was from another street in

40

Calle 'E.' I had heard of Edith, but when I asked her who lived in Calle 'E,' she said, "You'll see!"

We finally found one of the addresses my mother was looking for. When she knocked, an old lady answered the door and almost dropped the potted plant she was holding.

"Is this an apparition?" She asked.

Edith lived next to our house in Boniato. She has deep, blue eyes, and gray cottony hair, like my grandmother. In town, she was known as "*la burguesa*," the epithet for a bourgeoisie. As a kid, I liked Edith and her grandson, Ivan, my best friend, because they loved to read and their house was the replica of a house that, even then, I considered part of the old Cuba. There was only one problem: my grandmother and Edith never got along; theirs was a feud that goes back for more than thirty years. You see, Edith named one of her pigs after my cousin Susana and my grandmother never forgave Edith for that because whenever she called Susana's name, the pig would come grunting at her feet from under the fence diving the properties.

Edith is now very old. She can hardly walk and that afternoon, seeing my mother, tears came into her eyes. In between sobs, she kept saying how glad she was to see my mother, and me.

"Oh dear," she stuttered, "you loved to borrow my Agatha Christie's mystery novels, remember?"

We sat in her cool living room and she asked us all sorts of questions. She had visited New York City in her teens, she told us, and in her nostalgia, she loved to think of those days. She offered me a glass of soda too sweet for my taste, but anything was better than my thirst. At the end of our visit, she asked my mother about her old house in Boniato.

"It looks fine," my mother said, "just as I remembered it."

But Edith knew better. The house was not like before; where she once grew coffee plants, guava trees and exotic flowers, there is now a goat that roams free and eats away at the little grass that's left.

"I've never been back, in ten years since Mario's death," she said. "Nor do I want to go back, too many memories."

Before leaving, I asked her about her grandson. Ivan currently lives in Caracas, hoping one day to make his final move to Miami. Doesn't everyone? She asked.

When we left, I could see Edith going back to her flowers, to her lonely existence and to her many memories. I told my mother the sadness I felt seeing Edith again.

"You'll get even sadder now," she said.

I asked her what the mystery was all about.

Frowning, she said: "We're going to your father's old house, a few blocks from here."

The house is in Calle 'E'. The family living there now had a vague memory of the previous owners, especially of my father, a skinny man with green eyes, as they recollected. Despite their many assurances that the house had not changed in thirty-one years, I couldn't help but notice the red and blue paint peeling off the wall, curling like a tight fist, the splintered trusses on the roof and the rotting trellis out on the porch. (Showing my home video of the house in Miami, my grandmother refused to believe she was seeing her old residence.)

I took some pictures, was shown around the house, and then we left.

"Your father's family was very poor but clean and your grandmother cleaned and scrubbed that house everyday. Your grandfather sold *durofrios* in a little green Jeep." Durofrios are flavored ice cubes. "I think he also sold coconuts!"

Suddenly, taken by countless horse-drawn carriages, bicycles and mopeds, and in a moment of reflection, my mother turned to me and commented that even after a few days in Santiago, at times, she'd look around and get lost and feel as if she'd never lived here.

"Am I making sense?" She asked me.

I shook my head, yes.

My parents met sometime in the winter of 1967. It was a time when the youth of Cuba were beginning to look at the outside world for reprieve from the constant and ever-stifling hands of the then-young Cuban Revolution. Castro had already made communism official. It was also a time when the first wave of Cubans began to leave the country. Families that had hitherto not known the word 'exile' were confronted with the sad reality that at least someone they knew had left to the United States, Europe, or somewhere else. Naïve, seductively charmed by the young Castro, the great masses of the proletariats went along with the new Marxist indoctrination, and the divisions that would sadly sunder Cuban society to this day, commenced.

My parents met at a dance, at a house in Santiago renown for having record covers thumb-tacked to the walls. According to the official story, my father saw my mother across the room and asked her to dance a *dansón*, a waltz and then some *guaracha*. Ah yes, I can hear the music; I can see the spark in their eyes. In 1968, my father's parents left to Miami, where they lived for a few months in the historic Freedom Tower before heading up north to New York City in search of better employment opportunities. He was left behind, as he was of military-service age, and an aunt of his was entrusted to his care. When he turned eighteen, he asked my mother, only seventeen years of age, to marry him. What was she to do? He had no family, no one to love him, really. They married in 1970, in Boniato, and a year later, March 9, I was born. My grandmother's sister, Cusa, deeded my mother a plot of land next to the house in Boniato as a wedding present and my father began to build a house with two bedrooms and a small bathroom—the rest was left unfinished even when we left Cuba eight years later. When we left, Cusa attempted to have the property deeded back to her but the government refused. The house was given to a family of peasants, who completed building the house and took claim of the remaining plot of land.

My parent's marriage was never a happy one. For one, they were young. If my parents ever saw each other at all, they fought bitterly. With time, my father turned to alcohol and women, and my mother, giving up, led a life of her own. They never divorced, since at that time it would have been almost impossible to leave Cuba as a separate couple—the Mariel boatlift incident or the desperate attempts by rafters to get to US soil in inner tubes and rickety boats was not yet fashionable.

I don't think my father has ever forgiven his family for leaving him. He was in his early twenties and I must have been no more than five years old, but I can't forget how often he came home from a hard day's work, open a bottle of rum and start crying whenever his melancholy overwhelmed his desire to live. In my childhood foolishness, once, sensing that he was about to start crying (probably my grandfather was about to join him, too), I opened the living room window and said, "Dad, look, my grandparents are coming from New York!" Immediately he leaped to his feet, rushed to the window and when he saw that no one was coming, he looked at me incomprehensibly, lost, and went to bed. After that, he went through the longest depression he had ever suffered.

My father's story is a sad one. When he saw his parents again in Miami now with a family of his own and a failing marriage, he did his best to reestablish the bond he'd yearn for so long, but it wasn't the same. Twelve years before had marked the end of a family and the beginning of another; they were now strangers to him, to themselves.

When I think of my father, I don't know if he's a victim in this sad tale of Cuba's adventure in communism, or a man simply in love with anguish. I've never known him to be happy. I've never seen him laugh. Probably next to my birth, that winter day of 1967 when he met my mother was one of the happiest days of his life, but his happiness must have been mixed with the bittersweet fear of what was to come. I will have more to say about this in my next chapter.

~   ~   ~

"That's where we met!" My mother said pointing at the house and eyeing it with hungry eyes. Could she hear the music—the Beatles, the Supremes? But the house was silent, vacant it seemed. When we were about to leave a woman came out to the porch and recognized my mother.

"You're Jorge's son, too! *Muchacho*, you're his spitting image!" She roared above crashing pots in the kitchen. The woman asked about my father, his family, and asked me to send her fondest greetings to everyone in Miami. "I hope we're all united one day, again," she said with a sigh. I smiled.

We thanked the lady and walked down boulevards and strange streets. For a woman who loves a good conversation, my mother was strangely quiet. I couldn't tell whether she was trying to remember something or lost in Santiago.

"Boy is it hot!" She kept repeating. "When I met your father, it wasn't this hot. It couldn't have been."

"Am I to believe that?" I asked in jest.

She looked at me.

"Do you know that when I met your dad, that woman you just met had been his date at the party?"

She smiled. My mother loves to play with the hands of destiny.

Boniato, April 23, 1979.

Dear Granny:
I've taken it upon myself to write since no one seems to want to write you any more. So, why not, I thought. My dad doesn't live with us any more, and he's been seeing another woman these last few months. That woman is a viper! You should see her. My dad has no time for me, can you believe it? The viper also has three daughters and my dad has very little to support me. I want you to come to Cuba and see for yourself. Something has happened to him. Maybe, just maybe, if you come, he will go back to being the way he was and love me. She's trash. If and when you come, don't forget to bring me nice things. I like toys but there aren't many and the ones I have I don't like. But you can bring me whatever you like. Well, I hope I haven't bothered you much with this letter. I hope I haven't things that will make you cry. Just remember that only you can change my dad. Why aren't you here with us? When you come, I will give you lots of kisses, I promise.
Your grandson, Jorgito.

"ACTOS DE REPUDIOS..."

(Acts of Repudiation)

In 1979, during '*El Mariel*' exodus, as it became known, my grandfather Bebo, sensing the opportunity of a lifetime, chartered a boat in Miami to pick us up in Cuba. Unfortunately, he sailed on the day of an approaching hurricane and halfway in his voyage, he was forced to turn back as the winds in the Florida straights threatened to capsize the boat. He arrived safe in Miami three days later, resolute not to attempt the perilous journey again.

My parents were disappointed and upset. This meant one thing: we had to stay in Cuba. My father couldn't understand what bad luck seemed to beset him, even families with distant relatives in the United States seemed to leave Cuba overnight—they just packed their bags one day and you never saw them again. Trying to find innovative ideas to leave Cuba, my father and a cousin of his came up with an idea: why not show up at the Mariel seaside in Havana to be deported as cross-dressers? Gay men were, after all, in the government's list of anti-social elements, '*lacras*' and they, along with hardened criminals, were forcibly sent by the Shiploads to the USA. My mother didn't like the idea and it was dropped. Her reasoning, of course, made sense: what if they were not believed? Everyone would start calling them '*locas*', queers, the worst insult a Cuban man could be called. They desisted, the Mariel boatlift ended, and we were still in Cuba.

My father, though, was determined to leave that hellhole, '*este infierno*' as he called Cuba. He befriended a Santeria priestess, a *santera*, who almost on a daily basis read to him his cosmic chart. When that didn't work, he asked my mother to have her aura cleansed—he figured she was the one with bad karma! When that, too, failed to achieve his desired results, I was taken to the santera just in case I was the bearer of bad luck—anything and everything to leave Cuba, whether that meant bribing the gods or cajoling

47

someone to speed our visas' arrival—it didn't matter. In many ways, I can understand him. The years were passing and his dream of reunification with his family turned into an obsession. Sure, from time to time, he received the occasional pictures, letters and gifts sent by my grandmother, but his craving to understand why they left without him and his inability to find any plausible answers always irked him, to this day. He would look at pictures and notice his family's changes, their new Americanized way of living. My aunts married men of Italian and German descent, not Cubans. The first time I saw my grandmother Elvin was in a picture where she is sitting on a sofa among family members and her face is inscrutable, enigmatic. Recognizing a family resemblance, I asked my father, "Is she my grandmother?" and he said, "Yes and she's beautiful," pointing to her blue eyes which so much resembled his.

The letters my mother wrote to my grandmother in the late 1960's have allowed me to understand a world I thought was hermetically sealed from me. At first, when my mother writes them, she is a teenager discussing about love, hope and destiny. Marriage is impending and my dad is looking forward to a future with his beautiful bride. A few years later, after I'm born, the letters take on a darker tone until my mother stops writing and then I take up the pen and begin asking my grandmother potentially threatening questions I never received replies to…

In 1982, our visas were approved to leave for the United States through a third country, Costa Rica, in six months' time. We were dumbfounded.

The oldest known picture of my grandfather,
Estanislao, taken sometimes in the 1920's.

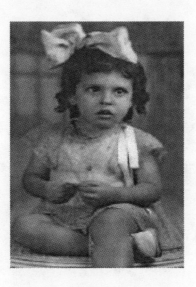

Even though she looks healthy and strong this picture of
Mimi was taken days before she was expected to die.

My grandparents and aunts still living at El Zaino, 1940's.
My mom had not been born yet.

This picture was taken in front of the Boniato house, my mother is the girl sitting on the
hood of the truck bearing the 'El Zaino' banner.

My grandmother, Elvin, holding my dad in 1949.

My dad, grandfather and aunts, 1958, standing
in front of the old Bacardi and Hatuey Beer brewery in Santiago.

My mother, Grisell Figueras, with my dad, Jorge Reyes, in courtship days, 1968.

My parents' wedding, in Boniato, 1970.
My grandparents are in the background, to the left.

Who's that baby?
Me, of course, only a few days old.

My grandfather and parents, 1972.

*The school's principal once told me I'd make a good communist,
to which I agreed, promising to be like Ché Guevara!*

After waiting for so long, after all the pain and the tears (and after my father's supposed stint with cross dressing) this seemed to be a joke. By now, my grandfather had passed away, but my grandmother wasn't and she didn't like it! It was bad enough that she'd already lost a daughter, Zuzel, without having to lose another one, her youngest one, and with her grandson on top of that! Unable to understand why my parents wanted to take me away from the people and things I loved—my cousins, my books, the chickens I raised and bartered—I made it clear that I did not want to leave. In school, I was exceeding everyday—I was second in the class. Why this sudden departure? Why now?

Up until that time, our friends and neighbors seemed supportive of our decision to leave to Cuba. Soon, though, word got out that our visas had arrived and one night, trying to concentrate with my geography home-work, I turned around and saw out the window what at first seemed to be a small group of people gathering in front of the park, right next to our house.

"Is there a carnival or something?" My grandmother asked.

"Looks like it, I guess it is," my mother said.

Not thinking anything about it, we went back to our chores when all of a sudden we heard loud thunderous applause, claps and chants: *Que viva Fidel! Abajo con los gusanos! Down with the worms, parasites!* We looked at one another in unbelief: what had originally been a small group turned out to be a massive gathering of about 100 people holding plac-ards, loudspeakers and effigies against us; it was an act of repudiation, '*actos de repudios,*' or well-orchestrated mass demonstrations fashionable at this time. Some of these repudios, as I recall, often turned ugly. One repudio in particular I remember was in another town called Santa Maria close to Boniato against a family of dissidents. My mother and I saw it happen from a cab on our way to Boniato, and I have never forgotten that day. The dissident, a simple, frightened man, was made to stand in front of a crowd and forced to endure insults and tirades, plus the occa-sional pebble he missed by docking sideways. Some in the mob were threateningly holding mangoes and ripe guavas, just in case the poor man provoked them. Imagine that!

Like a lioness, my mother dashed out to the patio. Sensing the futility of arguments, my grandmother begged her not to stoop to their level.

"Come back, *hija*, please, don't run the risk, shame them with your silence."

My mother looked at us, then for a very long time she looked searchingly into my eyes, until she walked back to the house, in defeat.

"You know what pisses me off," she said as she heard the chants, *Pin pan pun, abajo la gusanera!*, "so many of my friends are out there!"

"Your friends?" My grandmother asked going back to her needlework. My mother, in silence, made herself a sandwich and watched as the night unfolded with its many screams. A week later, she ran into the house to tell us she'd been chased by a general repudio in Santiago. But that wasn't all. Days later when my father came we noticed a bump on his forehead—someone had thrown a mango at him on his way home.

"This country is going to the pits!" He said, in shock. "I have pity on anyone who stays behind."

On a late January day, my father came by the house. My mother and Mimi were waiting for him. Whistling, he went to the bedroom and started to pack the few shirts he owned. When he finished packing, he looked around the house, making a mental image of every corner, every picture, every piece of furniture. Unceremoniously, he kissed my mother and Mimi. He then patted me on the head and said, "You'll thank me one day." With a slim bag slung on his back, not once looking back at us, he walked to the bus stop with a sprightly gait not before being spotted by a neighbor who blurted out from inside his house, '*Al fin!*' at long last! My father waved at the man. His dream had come true. He was the same age I am now.

When we went back in the house, my grandmother was in the living room busy at work with her needlework, humming a song, '*Delgadina,*

Delgadina, no me entierren por los igos que han faltado.' She looked at us three and lowered her face feigning concentration.

From the shadows of my memories, I see a moon. Mimi and I are sitting on the steps of the house, us alone, holding hands, afraid. The year is 1982 and fourteen years have passed since Mimi has seen her own children, Mildred and Arturo. By now they are grown adults, not the kids she remembers-she's now a grandmother. She knows her kids love her and want to see her…though she can feel, sense in their voices when she speaks to them on the phone, that time can be cruel. She's very skeptical about the future. The best thing for her now, as the day of our departure approaches, is fortitude and stoic discipline, which is why she's afraid. The world is a scary place, she knows…

As for me, I see the moon. Dogs bark in the distance like wailing ghosts. Crickets chirp with a melody that only the night understands. Alone, my grandmother is inside the house watching her *novelas* or maybe the late night news—Jimmy Carter, the one who allowed the Mariel boatlift, is no longer president of the United States but an actor from Hollywood is, a Ronald something, an actor who hates communism and called it evil. If my grandfather were alive, he would have been proud of this Ronald.

"You won't forget me, will ya?" Mimi asks me.

"No, no *tia,* of course not, how can I?" I retort, insulted.

"Well, it happens, people forget to write."

"But I won't, I love you a lot."

She smiles. Her dark eyes are ablaze.

"I will tell you how not to forget me, you want to know how?"

I come closer, hold her hands tighter. Of course I want to know.

"But first you must promise me one thing, *hijo.*"

"Anything," I say about to place my fisted hands to my chest, like Ché.

"You must promise me this: as soon as you get to Miami, call my children in Los Angeles and tell them how much I love them…"

"Yes…"

"…and you must tell them that I will see them one day…promise me that."

"I promise."

"Good."

I wait. The world seems to stand on the brink of silence in response to the secret she's about to impart on me.

"Now I can tell you how not to forget me, or us, your family. Look…look at the moon, look at it close. See her face tilted, sad almost, like a mother's face?"

I shake my head.

"Her face is the same everywhere and it never grows old. *Hijito lindo*, look at the moon and remember this poor aunt of yours, remember us in Cuba, don't forget us, not even when you are an old shriveled man, *un viejito chocho*. The moon will never leave your side. "

I remember looking at the moon with Mimi for a long time before my memories halt with the slow, approaching celestial movements of clouds. We hold hands. We look ahead.

My mother allowed me to have the window seat on the plane that day. She didn't want to look out. I did, and I saw my aunts, Mimi, Lisette and Dalcis, plus my cousins, standing on the roof of Santiago's Airport. They were all still young and looking ahead for the day we could be reunited. It was a beautiful January day. The night before I said goodbye to my grandmother, whose wails I could hear even from outside the house. Soon, we are flying over clouds. I wave goodbye at my family as I see them turn into small running ants, but they can't see my small hands desperately wanting to touch them from such a great distance.

"They were waving goodbye at me," I said to my mother. "Didn't you see them?"

"Yes, of course I saw them," she answers, sternly. Is she mad? I wonder.

From such great altitude, I try to spot the house in Boniato, but of course couldn't find it in that map of the world outside—there were only greenish mountains thinly veiled by passing clouds and a vast blue ocean that stretched on all sides of my periphery. I then try to look up at the sky and to my surprise, I notice that the sky isn't blue at all, but purple, and the more I look at it, the darker the sky became. Why was I so intent on looking at the sky that day? Who knows. Perhaps I was trying to find vultures carrying away the dead. One thing was for sure: the sky was vast, without a beginning or an ending, a thing to fear, a thing to marvel at. Soon, there was no earth or mountains to see, and soon even clouds disappeared since we were flying so high.

In an hour or two, we'd be in Havana, where my father was waiting for us. In a flash, we left our past —the only world we ever knew—to a world unknown. It all happened so suddenly.

~ Part 2

SANTERIA

My personal experiences with the Santeria religion have been funny rather than profound. My grandfather, who feared the occult, was a devout believer. He was also a partygoer, and Santeria offered him a change to revel in *bembés*—or rowdy religious celebrations that were anything but subdued. Once, my mother and grandfather took me to a bembé. My mother was genuinely interested to know when we would leave Cuba while my grandfather was interested in only one thing: to know when that SOB (Castro, of course) was going to die. At first that night, nothing out of the ordinary happened but soon the bembé took a dramatic turn. You see, after a few hours, the devotees got drunk with homemade *aguardiente* rum and what was supposed to be a simple religious ceremony culminated in a loud, boisterous party of flicking machetes, strangely sensuous rumba dances and simulated sexual practices. Horrified, my mother took me home earlier than expected. My grandfather stayed until the end.

When my grandfather died, the consensus around the house was that it was time to contact him—our failure to have done this sooner was unforgivable. So my family invited a santera, Alina, who was also the local math teacher, to channel his spirit. Since I wasn't sure what was going to happen during the séance and probably still traumatized about my previous experiences with bembés, the night of the séance I hid behind the curtains. I was just like my grandfather—I was terrified of the occult.

"Alina, please help us," said my grandmother when Alina came that night. "I don't want him to feel neglected by us. As it is, we've already seen two apparitions of him." My grandmother pointed at me shivering behind the curtains. Earlier that week, I had boasted at having seen my grandfather's shadow.

Alina shook her head, sat in her chair, closed her eyes and after a few minutes her face went pale as her lips and nostrils quavered. Soon, she began to jump in the chair and then with a raspy voice, she unrolled a few expletives. Whom had she channeled? By the sound of her voice, it sounded as if she were speaking French or some African dialect. But then, breaking the magic spell, my grandmother got up from her chair.

"What's this?" she asked.

Alina went silent, got up too and without speaking or looking at any of us, her eyes watered—my grandfather loved to cry. My grandmother, surprised, cleared her voice. "Chichito…is that you?" She asked using my grandfather's nickname.

"Belica, yes, who else *vieja?*"

Shocked, holding her rosary, she sat back in the chair. "Well…I'll be darn…"

My 'grandfather' started to talk about many things that made little sense to me. Everyone, though, seemed to be genuinely impressed by Alina's psychic powers. In the middle of her séance, subdued and calm at first, Alina began to limp like my grandfather had done when he left to the hospital for the last time. Her arms curled like a cripple and she shuffled her leg. By now she looked like a very old woman not the feared math teacher that she was.

Silence reigned in our small living room; we were fastened to her every word, to her every physical movements. At one point, growing beet-red in the face, she asked for a cigar. "Of course, of course, quick, quick, anybody, give her a cigar, give her one!" my grandmother screamed. "It's Chichito!"

But then, without warning, another spirit took possession of Alina and in a fit of passion, she started to roar and yell. My aunts began to cry and I, spooked out of my mind, ran to hide under the bed to pray. I don't know how long I hid under the bed when, suddenly, everyone began to look for me.

"Find him, find Jorgito and quick!" Thundered my grandmother as Alina, by now, was howling like a dog. Something wrong had happened!

When I came out of hiding, I will never forget what I saw: Alina was naked from the waist up. In one of her fits with an evil spirit, she had ripped her blouse to shreds and had flung her bra across the room. Worst still, she was now demanding *aguardiente*, beer and more cigars. She wanted to rumba! She wanted to frolic with a man! By the look on my grandmother's face, I could tell she had not counted on this demonic turn-of-events.

~   ~   ~

On my third day in Cuba, I was told to visit a santero. Of course, I agreed. As most Cubans know, a santero divines the future, often trying to divert the fateful hands of destiny by supplications, if not outright bribery, to the gods. While I was waiting to be consulted, he was telling a woman on the best ways to bring back her beloved: a bath of herbs and honey, and a couple of prayers a day. This, he assured her, plus his own prayers, would guarantee a satisfactory ending to her love problems. A young man, high-strung and nervous, wanted to leave the country. After much consultation with cowrie shells and with his usual self-assurance, the santero predicted two ways out for the young man: one, to marry a foreigner or two, to win the national immigration lottery which currently grants 20,000 visas each year to Cubans. As far as the shells spoke, of the two choices, the most probable one would be by way of marriage. Among many things the young man was instructed to do, one was to make a little female doll made of yarn and pray to it every day and another was to take the usual bath of herbs—with, yes, honey. The young man promised the santero he'd be back in two days with herbs, the doll, plus $2 for *Changó*.

Every santero in Cuba has an altar dedicated solely to the 'powers.' The altar for this particular santero was a table covered by a white sheet, topped with myriad cups filled with small crosses submerged in water. The consultation room was decorated with a collection of black dolls dressed in white, as well as an unusual array of saint figurines: Santa Barbara, San

Lazaro, San Judas Tadeo, and an Indian statute he said represented "the African potencies." On top of the altar, there was a huge eye, "to protect one's self against the evil eye."

Typically, after throwing cowrie shells on the floor, a santero interprets the message, telling you, first, that you're the son/daughter of this or that saint. So, if you're a progeny of Santa Barbara (Changó), you're a warrior, always carrying the sword, always ready for a good fight. (I was the son of Obalatá.) He told me that I had a great future, but that I was a dreamer, the reincarnation of a martyred priest in my previous life.

I asked him why was it that santeria had been unable to change Cuba's "problem." All of a sudden, he stopped, clamped tight the plug of cigar he was chewing, and told me that *He* had more protection and powers, *aché*, than anyone else alive today. *His* forces were indestructible. Without mentioning names, I knew whom he was referring to, Fidel. And with that, he went on with my reading. After his reading, he asked me not to forget him and write him once all the prophecies for me had come true. He also recommended us to visit the Shrine of Cuba's patron saint, La Virgen de la Caridad del Cobre.

Little did I know until after I got back to Miami that my mother had followed the santero's advise and conned Lisette to help her find all the herbs she needed for a 'cleaning.' What I didn't know until much later was that the car used to get her around the city ran out of gas in one of the worst neighborhoods of Santiago and my mother, Lisette, the driver and half a dozen men had to push the car around the city for about an hour until they got home. No wonder she had such nice tan when we left Cuba!

That same day, I visited the shrine of La Virgen. It wasn't easy to get to El Cobre town because no cars were available. The church sits atop a mountain in El Cobre next to a quarry, close to El Zaino. by an enclosing iron fence. People from all over the world come to see this religious and historical icon, bringing flowers, candles, pictures, and gold offerings that are then enclosed in large glass panels for display. When my parents left Cuba, my mom offered the saint her wedding band in appreciation for allowing us to leave the country. The statue is on the second floor, where pictures are not allowed, though I took one.

Outside the church, peddlers sell little replicas of saints carved in wood. I bought one for $2.00 dollars. Other peddlers sell you little pieces of stone, flowers, candles and rosaries. A black man with dreadlocks and a bead necklace offered me some of his special stones free, for good luck, as he said, since heavenly benediction is never for sale. Politely I bought the stones for .25 cents.

Probably, around the time I write this, the santero is still there, divining people's destiny in his modest apartment. The sun is probably setting behind the mountains, and Santiago, in this hazy afternoon of tropical breeze, must be hot and humid, alive behind the seeming weariness of its people, a people questioning an unknown tomorrow despite the god's ceaseless attempts to guide them.

FIDEL

By now I'd been in Cuba for six days. I was resting in Boniato when a friend of the family came by to meet us. After we were introduced, I apologized and told him that I was curious to watch Fidel's speech on TV.

"May I watch it with you?" He asked.

"I don't mind, by all means."

I turned the TV on and a faded, color flicker came on. Belkys sat next to me, opened a pack of cigarettes, lit a cigarette and began to scrutinize our reaction to Fidel's speech.

"Will you look at *him!*" The young man said. "At his age, shouldn't he retire or something?"

~   ~   ~

'Fidel! Fidel.' The voices blared and blended above cheers. *'Fidel!'* was about to make a speech. A man in green fatigues, a man in control of his world, of his destiny, waved against a resplendent dusk. It wasn't an ordinary man the man who waved; it was *the* man, the man whose name was on everyone's lips. A shiny deluge of red hankies were raised against the sky and the man, *'Fidel!'* waved, smiled, not a bead of sweat on his brow, not even when he cupped his hands over his eyes so he could see them, the masses—*his* people—and suddenly it was rapture, heaven on earth on this July day, as he started to give one of the many speeches in commemoration of the beginning of the revolution. He was the man alright! *'Fidel!'* the name on everyone's lips; *'Fidel!'* the name everyone recognized; *'Fidel!'* the man everyone loved, if not because they were afraid not to fear him...

'Fidel!' finished his speech. It was getting late and everyone was tired. In over five hours, *'Fidel!'* had spoken about everything there was to speak about and everything there was to know about life: love, politics, philosophy, literature, anything; and even then the man didn't seem satisfied. The

longer he spoke the more energy he seemed to get. Whence he got this energy, no one knew. At times, he winked, tired, too, perhaps. At times, he looked at the gulf of dark heads looking up at him as if to a god. At times, he finger-pointed at the horizon, to the enemy that existed anywhere out there, somewhere. At times, he puckered his lips, pressing a delicately manicured finger to his lips. At times, he stopped talking, listening, perhaps, to the voices trapped in the wind. At times, he looked up at the sky, perhaps trying to see the vision he'd sought so long to behold, although there was nothing to see. The man, now, seemed to be introspective, by himself, unmindful of the masses, the dark masses shivering in the cold with red hankies in their laps. He put his glasses on; he was having trouble seeing. He'd been speaking for too long and he seemed confused, old age, perhaps, his strangely pale face a mask of worry. The man caught a glow from an overheard light and he heard the far away chanting '*Fidel!*' and he recognized the name and he came alive, for he knew it was him they were calling. He looked down after such a long speech and said, 'Socialism or death, Fatherland we shall overcome!' '*Fidel!*' had finished his speech.

The man's eyes were weary. That much I could see that day, the day I saw him. He smelled of rum and sweat, and he was tired. He'd been speaking for many days. He needed the silence, at least for a few hours. If only he could fall asleep and dream, but he had not dreamed in years, it frightened him to dream, so many voices fought for his attention in his dreams. The car rolled over a crag of rocks and he hit his head with the jolt. *Coño*, he thought. He relit a cigar, deep in thought. When he opened his eyes, the car's tinted window seemed to tint the noonday outside with darkness. Good. No one could see him now.

The smoke hung thick in the car. When someone, the chauffeur, began to sneeze the man realized he was not alone. 'Don't worry,' he said, 'the smoke will go away,' and eyeing the chauffeur with curiosity, he continued to smoke rolling the well-chewed cigar slowly on his lips. 'Where are we going?' He asked, at a loss, dreamily, and the chauffeur told him they were heading to El Cristo, near Boniato, to open a day care facility on this day of Ché's passing. The man turned around and saw an entourage of jeeps following. He shook his head appreciatively and rolled the window halfway down, 'There you go, so you won't asphyxiate,' and the cigar smoke flew out into the clear of the sky. 'Thank you, Commander,' said the chauffeur. Breaking the awkwardness of the moment, he continued, 'Look how nice they look, the little pioneers, just like Ché would have wanted,' and the man with weary eyes shook his head as if slowly awakening from a dream.

The car made a sharp turn on a street corner in Boniato and the man saw a group of pioneers hurling flowers to the river. 'How nice, you're right...look...look, just like Ché!' The chauffeur adjusted the rear view mirror and said, 'But of course just like Ché, how silly...' and he stopped, afraid, but the man with weary eyes, letting his white effeminate hand dangle over the half-open window and chewing the stub of his cigar, was amazed, mesmerized, that all the children, *his* pioneers, were waving good-bye at him and chanting *Fidel! Fidel!*

I was one of those children, my first and only encounter with Fidel.

When I went home that day, my grandmother was already waiting for me with a glass of *café con leche*; my grandfather was watching TV, hoping I wouldn't say anything about who I had seen. Nothing was said of Ché or of Fidel!

~   ~   ~

Hours later, restless by Fidel's monotonous speech and unable to restrain himself, the young man started to ask me what kind of publicity *El Barbudo*, the bearded-one, (Fidel, like Changó, goes by many names) received in Miami. I told him that due to the influx of Cubans into South Florida, information about Cuba or Fidel was abundant, and that while nothing positive was ever reported about him in the two local Spanish stations, usually, not often, a national TV station would run news documentaries on Fidel focusing on the struggle of the Cuban nation. I gave him a particular instance where CBS news anchor, Dan Rather, produced a sympathetic hour-long documentary on Fidel and the revolution, getting even a personal guided tour of the Sierra Maestra Mountains by none other than Fidel himself.

Somehow, the conversation got heated when one of my aunts, a sympathizer of the revolution, commented that she was glad that Chile's Pinochet had been arrested, he was a common, two-bit dictator, unlike Fidel, who's defiance of Uncle Sam was admirable. She was testing us. I didn't join in the lively discussion. But, I had to admire them both. My aunt, well meaning that she is, for thinking that the end justifies the mean, and he, frightened and cowed, for defending principles that could have easily landed him in jail.

The 1959 Cuban Revolution, by far, is Fidel's Revolution. His image, his voice, is everywhere. There are more posters, broadsides, books, pamphlets of him and written by him than of any other person in Cuba, with the exception of Martí and then Ché. He is infallible, revered. He's a romantic, with a strangely dark side to him, revengeful, vindictive, even cruel, according to one biographer. There are some who still remember Fidel's student days and recall that he was once married to the heiress of a great family fortune and that they had a son, Fidelito. In Miami, you can still hear of some old-timer who, with a mixture of pride and guilt, boasts to have met him once, often on intimate terms. One of my Spanish teachers in school would often tell us that *he* was a classmate of *hers* at the University of Havana, and she always remembered how he would rip off the pages of textbooks after reading them and, to prove his intelligence, quote from them verbatim. This is probably all myth, but this is the myth that has sustained him for forty years.

I never knew what to make of Fidel, then or now. Coming from a family whose opinions of him were, at best, mixed, I never felt the hatred that his name conjures among many other Cubans of my same background. I know that my grandfather hated him. As I wrote, I was forbidden to bring his name up in any of my afternoon classes, and for men like my grandfather, I can be nothing but sympathetic. As late as the 1960's—way after Fidel said in a speech flanked by bearded rebels, smiling women and an admiring throng of people—that he would be a communist for the rest of his life, my grandfather had great hopes for our country and its new government. His discontent, surprisingly, didn't begin when El Zaino was confiscated (he was left with three cows, one of which was still alive when I was born, a mare, $100 and an arid plot of land), but when his oldest daughter, Zuzel, left for Puerto Rico. After that, Mimi's kids left with their father, and from then on, sisters, daughters, neighbors began to leave for that great country that now Castro despised so much. Those who were left behind could only dream of the possibilities of reunification with those whom the government now called 'worms,' 'parasites,' and 'mafia,' sometime in the future—that great future that may come too late! Personally, my grandfather could never understand what inner demons could drive a man who seemed to have such personal distaste for anyone who disagreed with him or his ideals. Whenever he would see Castro on TV touting the wonders of socialism, he would only have to think of my father's loneliness and misery and say that no system was worth defending if it was immune to the suffering of one man.

My grandparents accepted their destiny and retired into a life of complacency. With their one last remaining cow, they would still make a meager living selling milk in the black market. But more often than not, sensing their dependency, they would look up at the sky in search of a benevolent God and question Him when this, communism, would be over. My grandfather particularly the older he got the more resentful he grew. And what was worse, some of my aunts were caught up in the charm and lofty ideals of communism and fell in love with Castro, going so far as to hang his pictures on walls, replacing wedding and baptism pictures. Strangely enough, though, Fidel's picture would often be found inside the toilet bowl, crushed to a ball. Little did my grandfather know that he would die and Fidel's smile with his scraggly beard would still be flying over buildings, schools and hospitals. In the end, he would sit in the porch of the house seeing how the garden his daughters tended dried like his dreams, how grass gave way to weeds and how sad and drab life was without those he'd known in the past.

Eventually, after Belkys and the young guy battled it out for about an hour, my mother and I decided to leave to my cousin Alex's house in Santiago, where we were going to spend the night. On our way there, I could hear Fidel's strangely tilting voice blaring out from radio sets and see his image on TV screens in empty living rooms. Since the 26th of July Memorial coincides with the carnival, and the Cuban people are so festive, many were waiting for his speech to end so that the carnival could begin. So much for the Cuban Revolution. So much for the New Man.

A few minutes past midnight, trying to get some sleep, I could hear the clamors and cheers of the people. Fidel's speech had ended! The carnival had begun!

~ ~ ~

The carnival and the celebrations of the revolution take place in the month of July. The carnival runs for an entire week and the people don't seem to tire from the uninterrupted daily celebrations. Everywhere you turn at this time of the year, you see kiosks made from palm fronds where beer, pizza, and if you're really lucky, *chicharrón*, pork rind, are sold. Music is everywhere, with small groups improvising songs with typical Cuban flare. Near the renown *El Encanto* store, one of these bands with five men dressed in red livery and straw-hats were rattling their *guayos*, *maracas* and playing their guitars to the sonorous tunes of a woman.

> *Cachita has gone nuts,*
> *Cachita's no longer here,*
> *Cachita's 'guarachando',*
> *Where has Cachita gone to?*

My cousin told me that Cachita was another name for La Virgen de la Caridad del Cobre, and this song, like everything else Cuban, was a subtle song of protest.

Going up Martí Boulevard, under a splendid noonday sun, large groups of people were dancing, singing and drinking, unmindful now of Fidel—or were they? Men and women, mostly black or mulatto, were dressed in gay carnival costumes. At times, I'd hear the voices of Madonna or Mariah Carey, though their voices and their songs dispersed quickly in an orgiastic air filled with deep guttural sounds and the throbbing sensual beats of maracas, gourds, conga drums. What a world! What a world Cuba is! What disparity!

GOODBYE, CUBA

Friday. In about a week in Cuba, I had lost about ten pounds. I was so exhausted that I didn't even get hungry. I just wanted to rest on my bed and sleep undisturbed with my own dreams and nightmares. For the last two days, my mother had been suffering from food poisoning. She refused to go to the hospital, and my cousin Karel tried to cure her by massaging her stomach with an ointment as he sang little ditties. She now looked pale and withdrawn. Zuzel was trying to put a good face to what, in a few hours, was inevitable: our leaving. This was our last day.

To celebrate, my family treated us to the most succulent suckling pig I've ever tasted. This, they assured us, was in our honor, for a family gathering would not be the same unless it culminates in a large banquet. The pig was bought from a peasant at El Cobre with a sour sop in its crisped snout. Two kegs of beer were also bought, and before we knew it, we were all sitting around the dining room table, enjoying the tasteful chunks of pig marinated with orange, lemon, tamarind leaves and vinegar, plus *congri*, yucca and *boniatillo* for dessert.

My grandmother was proud to sit at the head of the table that day, very proud. I don't think she had been that happy in many years, joined by her six daughters and a slew of grandsons, great-grandsons, cousins and nieces, and the usual drop-ins of friends.

I was asked many times when I would come back, my younger cousins in particular, who were enthralled by my 'Spanglish', my accent, and anything that I said about *El Norte*. My grandmother, opening up, sent kisses to her family in Miami, telling them by name that she loved them and missed them. My cousins wished that their other cousins would visit one day, as I had done. Older family members sent greetings to particular relatives they remembered fondly. Soon, the house was filled with laughter, all of us talking at once, reminiscing about yesteryears, until, after many

75

swigs of beer, no one cared about anything other than the present moment. We were having a good time, Cuban style.

Karel proposed to play a CD I bought at the dollar store, but the idea was at first shut down by my aunts, in respect of granny's illness, though she shook her head to say that she, too, wanted to hear some music.

"What's that new music called?" She asked. "Disco?"

I asked my grandmother to show me old pictures and she handed me three small boxes full of pictures. I skimmed through them, one by one, seeing the years go by with a quick glimpse. She would often point at particular pictures: a picture of her sister, Marianita, who passed away from TB in the 1930's; pictures of her parents—two very old pictures that seemed to disintegrate by my touch; pictures of my mother; pictures of my aunts in lacy dresses; pictures of Mimi and her adopted mother, Rosilla the Cow. My grandmother was particularly happy to show me pictures of me growing up as a little kid riding a bicycle in Hialeah; mountain hiking in Costa Rica; going off to college; graduating from college. She'd seen me grow from afar.

Pictures. What would our concept of memory and time be without them? Our century is a tale of pictures, milliseconds caught and preserved, seized and arrested with a smile, or with a tear. Pictures. The town of Boniato in its infancy. Our house nothing more than concrete and mortar. My mother with friends over a birthday cake. Pictures. My grandmother, my grandfather, my five aunts and my baby mother smiling for the future, this future, my present, sitting around one of the Royal Poinciana trees in the park—the same trees I was looking at from the living room bending at the whim of a slight breeze.

My aunt, my mother and I were to leave at four. The bus was slated to depart for Holguín at five. None of us dared say the dreadful words, *it's time to leave*, until I motioned my mother with my head and she, in turn, motioned to my aunt Zuzel.

My grandmother, knowing that we were communicating with our eyes, bent her head slowly and looked out the window to an afternoon sun that glared in her dark eyes. Children in the park were taking turn on the merry-go-round, on the swing, some were playing hopscotch with a flattened tin can. She puckered her lips, looked back at us and frowned. Were we an apparition to her? A glint from a past?

Twenty years before, we'd been roaming nervously around the same living room with the same freezer whirring in the background, the same pictures of swans on a pond hanging crookedly on the wall, sitting on the same chairs, drinking from the same cups, when my mother, sensing that delaying the inevitable was foolish, asked me to grab a little bag with my personal stuff. It was time to say goodbye. She kissed my grandmother and said reassuringly, "Don't worry, I'll come back soon, one day."

My grandmother asked us to help her to a corner in the living room where there was box. She asked me to open the box and when I did, to my pleasant surprise, I saw my old 1927 encyclopedia, *El Tesoro de la Juventud,* the same encyclopedia I used to help me assemble my lovechild, Fefita, more than twenty years before.

"I've kept it for you," she said, "for the day you'd come back. I haven't let anyone read it, borrow it, or even browse through it."

I opened one of the books, browsed through pages with beautiful renditions of paintings. I stopped on a section devoted to the tales of the Arabian nights and ran my finger along the sentences, sensing, again, the undiluted pleasure of my childhood days when the world was new and strange and words were the only medium of my imaginative escapades. In twenty years, I had changed so much, done so much, seen so much in that world only 90 miles away, and nothing in here—nothing at all—had changed. My name was scribbled, dated and inscribed on the first page. The inscription read, *"This book is property of Jorge. Should you find it if it is ever lost, you are under a moral obligation to return it to me to the following address..."*

When I looked up, everyone was saying good-bye. One of my cousins picked up the box and asked me to kiss my grandmother, but please, he said, only a quick kiss, she'd begun to sob. I got my backpack, put on a cap, slipped on a pair of sunglasses, gave my grandmother a kiss and said, "*Adiós, abuelita.*" I looked in her eyes, and her eyes expressed a sadness I will never forget.

That afternoon we left to Santiago in a clacking 1953 Plymouth Ford that skidded and glided down the slopping bridge of Quintero. A man by the name of Pancho who did nothing but chew a plug of cigar was the driver. He was trying to convince us to come back soon.

"As I see it, Cubans *over there* should never forget Cuba. It's so sad to see this thing about family being separated," he said.

My aunt asked him why she should return after... she didn't finish her sentence. She opened her arms as if to say, look around, what's left of my Cuba?

"Your family is here and they'll never change, they will always welcome you even if they hardly know you anymore." Truer words could not have been spoken.

From the jitney, our sad city looked as strange, as unfamiliar to us as on the first night we arrived. The carnival was in full swing and the people looked tired, lost. As usual, it was a hot and humid day, with a cloudless sky often shadowed by a flock of birds. My mother, with a lump at her throat, was holding back tears. My aunt, puckering her lips, was stifling her sobs. Trying to calm them, I began to talk about the beauty of our country, how tall were the mountains! how dark was the soil! They shook their heads, pretending to listen, though their thoughts, I knew, were somewhere else. Driving past Vista Alegre and going up a ramp to a highway, I kept hearing a persistent honking behind the jitney. Two of my cousins were following us in a car, flailing their arms out the window. My aunt and mother started waving, hoping that my cousins could catch a glimpse of them from inside the tinted windows. My mother pressed her hands flat against the glass-tinted window. One of my cousins fisted his hands in a symbol of solidarity:

they could see us. The jitney took speed on the empty expressway, overtaking my cousin's little white car which receded further and further until it became an infinitesimal point in the horizon.

At the airport in Holguín, a customs officer asked me to step aside and open the box of books. I opened it and he started to browse through the encyclopedia, page after page, scrutinizing anything that might look suspect. What was he expecting to find? I wondered. A missive against Castro? A plan to topple the government? Surprising even me, he pulled out an old love letter from Cusa, dated 1937. He handed it to me.

"Is there a problem?" I asked.

"Maybe," he said arching his eyebrows. "This encyclopedia is very old."

I arched my eyebrows, too. So? I meant to say.

He asked me to take a seat and wait for him. An hour later, he returned telling me that I couldn't take the encyclopedia out of Cuba, it was national patrimony, a national treasure. I was shocked. This is mine, I wanted to say, but more than mine, it's my grandmother's. He shook his head, called five more customs officers, and after fifteen minutes of consultation, the decision was still the same: the encyclopedia belonged to the people.

I looked at my mother. She shrugged her shoulders and asked me to sit with her to wait. Undaunted, I asked the customs officer if I could rip the first page of one of the books with my childish name written on it, Jorge Ivan Reyes Figueras, 1-29-78. He ripped the page, I thanked him, and went to sit with my mother and aunt.

"Don't worry, *hijo*, we'll be home in an hour," my aunt said. "Besides, you have a much better encyclopedia in Miami."

A hot vapor enveloped me. I looked out at the tarmac and beyond at the dark bushes of Holguín. My thoughts were racing. I thought of the vacated mansion in Vista Alegre, forlorn and decaying, symbol of so much destruction; of my mother's disillusion, of her alienation; of the sundering of the Cuban family; and I understood why so much hostility between Cubans existed and why this incident, trivial as it may seem, underscored the tragic reality of a Cuba that has been lost with all its treasures and all its beauty.

The three of us sat together, afraid, tired, disconcerted. It had been a long, tiring journey and what at first had seemed exuberant was now something we wanted to finish, and quickly.

We boarded the plane near midnight. In forty-five minutes we'd be in Miami. Unlike the first night on the airplane, my mother, my aunt and I dropped on our seats, noticing the neon sign of the Frank País Airport glowing against the darkness of Holguín.

"Just remember *who* we did it for," my aunt Zuzel said patting us in our hands.

They fell into a sweet slumber and I rested my head on my seat. The cushion felt comfortable as my eyelids fluttered tiredly. The deafening sound of the airplane lulled my mind. To think that behind me, under all that darkness, I was leaving behind so much history, so much of myself. I fought my sleep and wrote a poem about my grandmother.

In a town with a name strange to me,
In a town flanked by many mountains,
Many rivers and countless brooks,
In a town with many gods,
Strange whispers of yesteryears,
In a town of old time beauty,
Greenish nature glorious shining,
Far away from all I know,
Was I born,
And you, grandmother,
Taught me lessons everlasting,
Words I still hear,
Even as you are no more,
Except in dreams,
Beloved Isabel,
Grandmother.

I opened my aunt's letter. The paper was old, the Victorian handwriting slanting forward hastily. The letter opened with the usual remarks of unrequited love and ended with an impassioned plea to love him until the day she died. I chuckled at the words. True to her words, my aunt never married and she died childless being cared for by Belkys.

The plane slowly taxied on the tarmac until it heaved itself up, leaving behind a dark land with sparse lights that seemed separated, disjointed. '*Yes*,' everyone seemed to say, '*this is Cuba, the Cuba of our memories, the Cuba of our dreams, the Cuba of our birth, the strangely seductive, always exotic land only 90-miles away from home.*' And we were gone. Perhaps forever. I closed my eyes and I could see them again: my aunts Mimi, Lissette, Dalcis and my cousins at Santiago's Airport waving good-bye at me as I look up at the sky, and discover that the sky isn't blue, but purple, and the more I look at it, the darker it becomes until it is pitch black. Black, black, black.

Forty-five minutes later, at 2:00 a.m., we were back at Miami's International Airport. Zuzel's daughter was waiting for us. She looked concerned, worried. I hardly had any energy to haul our empty *gusanos*. She didn't ask us many questions. There would be plenty of time to inquire about Cuba, the Cuba of the past, our Cuba, some other time, tomorrow, perhaps.

As I look back now to that night, I find it amusing that neither my mother nor my aunt could talk, or would talk, or had the energy to talk. We got into her car, its smooth ride lulled my mind and I thought I was being drawn into the magical dream of sleepiness from which I would not return. I chuckled. This had been quite an adventure. The city lights of Miami engulfed us and we went home, my home.

EPILOGUE

Childhood memories are so unreliable. It seems like my family's history is a hybrid of tales being muted by the hands of time. No fiber that holds together that personal idea of identity that makes me Cuban, or American, or Cuban-American, exists. Whenever I feel part of one or the other, I am reminded that other parts are still disjointed, wanting to be reclaimed. Cuba is not a place to discover identity, now I know, but an ideal; a small part of me, one of many.

My identity is hearsay, a casualty in this war of words and ideals. Yes, I am proud to be who I am. I am proud to live where I do and represent what I represent—whatever that may be. And yet, I fear that there will be no Cuba to reclaim, no Cuba that to the evanescing memories of my family living in "*el exilio*" still exists pristine and pure in the warm stretch of the Caribbean. This is my nostalgia: that deep down there is no home for any of us. Should we ever go back, in this dream of many, we will always be nomads trying to conquer what no longer exists. As far back as my high school days, I wrote a poem about this sense of displacement that for some obscure reason I kept. It reads like this:

Pilgrim,
Lost in a world strange,
Gypsy,
Destitute in a crowd alone,
Nomad,
Homeless in a home not yours,
Unfurl the bellying sails,
The many seas await you,
Inhale the air that's briny,
A new adventure anew begins,
With a hope that exhilarates

Every time you say,

Pilgrim, gypsy, nomad.

This is what is like to be Cuban. This is my identity. This is my nostalgia.

We've gone to great lengths to say *we,* the exiles, speak for the truth, blinding ourselves to years that make us a bit older, a bit grayer and a lot more forgetful. Oh yes. We still talk about our homeland as if it were something permanent and inconsequential to an assimilation that eventually makes us more apathetic, a bit bitter, and in the end, never the same. Do we expect to find the same homes? The same cars? The same people? Yes and no. The gardens of our dreams have large splotches of dry grass. Our former homes, our former cars, our former nation is caught in a historical game from which no one comes out unscathed. Yes, I understand my mother and her alienation; I guess she saw the passing of time with tragic eyes; I guess she felt her own mortality in subtle of ways: unconsciously.

As I grow older and look back, my childhood memories are little things, mind you, personal touches. Strange even to me, I tend to look back and remember my third birthday party. My aunts, my parents and Edith with her grandson Ivan are standing in the back of a couch as I sit in my grandmother's laps for a picture. *Snap!* A picture is taken. *Snap!* We all smile for the future. What else do I see? Where is my memory taking me? I see a two-year old who's just dropped his pacifier to the river as his young parents try to steady him on the railings of a bridge. Now I'm six, my mother and I are in a conga, a large group of people are dancing, drinking, dancing, their ragged clothes wrapped around their heads, dancing, wide-hipped mulatto women swing sensuously, dancing, the beat of a tambourines and conga drums fervently disturbing the night with primeval longing. Everyone is dancing, dancing, dancing some more. The streets of Santiago grow dim. The smell of beer and urine permeate the night, unlike the gardenia in my grandmother's garden. Some people are dressed like clowns, '*mamarrachos.*' Older women from 'El Grillo', 'Chicharrón' 'Marti' neighborhood sport their starched white cotton petticoats with blessed, multicolored beads around their necks for the 'powers' as they sing in unison, "*Get ready here comes Cocoyé*". My mother holds my hands and she sees one of my aunts, wild and drunk, and we dance up cobblestone streets that have changed very little, or none at all, since the 18th century. I'm six years old, a pioneer enjoying a short reprieve from my responsibilities to the revolution in this orgy of camaraderie and African enchantment. By the time we get home, way past midnight, my grandmother is waiting for us. She doesn't like our staying out that late. She doesn't like our carousing with the rabble. She doesn't like it one bit.

This is my nostalgia. Time trapped. Time stopped. This is Cuba. This is what it means to be Cuban. A childhood memory. An old man's tear. To long for something that is no longer. To wish for a paradise that may be, after all, a myth.

~   ~   ~

I often wonder why I have so much interest in Cuba. Part of the answer, I think, lies in me, in my very being. I see America, with its countless different accents and myriad shades of colors, and I see Cuba, with its strange argot and affable classless paradise, through the bifurcated eyes of a 'Cuban-in-exile.' Cuba, 90 miles away, is a brief glance at a mishmash of black-and-white pictures of my mother's baptism, her sisters' weddings, and childhood picnics. What exists for her and for others like her are memories that become less reliable with the passing of time and whose nostalgia, I, too briefly embraced. I think it was Hemingway who said that memory is hunger.

And here lies the irony of my personal division: Miami with its 'latinized' flavor is the only world I truly know and Cuba, sad to say, is a strange land, as strange as on the day I arrived.

So, what did I rediscover? What was there to rediscover?

I went back to the source of my existence expecting to find an oracle that would explain the nature of my hyphenated being, but what I found instead was a puzzling labyrinth that left me with more questions than answers. Where was the Cuba of my grandparents' dreams? the paradise where the sea was the bluest, where the sand was the whitest, and where life was all the more simple. Writing these words, I still wonder.

Not too long ago, a friend of mine told me that the key to unraveling the uniqueness of our existence is to transcend the divisions within our world, reinvent ourselves and this is no different from any other immigrant group slowly assimilating the richness of another culture, slowly bastardizing the magic of our grandparents' dreams. Time, like Edith feared, can be a blessing and a curse. What remains of the Cuba I hear about are its people, a people as warm and hopeful as they've ever been. Ultimately, I think, it is this empathy for their welfare, that summons us Cuban-Americans to Cuba in spite of the years, in spite of the ever-changing ethnic, racial and economic landscape of present day Cuba, in spite of our own assimilation even. What remains of Cuba is the hope of a tomorrow unsullied by broken promises and maniacal revolutions that circumspect the very hope of our existence. When and how that happens remain to be seen.

~ ~ ~

Shortly after our return, a month later, my grandmother passed away.

The phone that night rang just like it did six months before. By the look on my mother's face, I could tell that something horrible had happened. Somehow, all of us were waiting for this moment but it seemed that nothing, absolutely nothing, could have prepared us for what we had been dreading: death, again. This time Dalcis called and she told us that within hours, they were expecting her death. I could see my mother closing her eyes, traveling to Boniato, going up the stairs of her old home, walking to her mother's bedroom, holding her hands, saying good-bye. I could see her there, not here. Her present was just a dream and her dream was her reality. Close to midnight we got the last call, she had passed away.

My grandmother was hastily buried the next day, next to my grandfather in Marimón (there's very little time to mourn in Cuba). Now, I can
look back and remember her the way I want to immortalize her in my
mind, an adult looking back with the eyes of a child, her kid, her doting
baby whom she smothered and pampered to her heart's content. From
now on, my grandparent's love for each other will be eternal, like my parents' dreams of Cuba. One day, I too will join them but perhaps far away
from both of them.

There are curious rumors relating to her death and funeral. A day
before she died, she asked every family member to stop trying to keep her
alive with oxygen masks and pills: she was ready to meet her maker. A few
hours before her death, she asked my cousin Karel to air a black dress she
kept in the armoire: she wanted to be buried in it. And yes, she was buried
the next day with that dress, holding the figurine of *La Virgencita* I had
bought her at *El Cobre*.

And that was the end. Old Cuba was disappearing. Nothing would ever
be the same. Two weeks later, my mother received a letter from Dalcis. In
it, she alluded to the encyclopedia. Apparently, my cousins had gone to
Holguín to reclaim it but the government would not release it—not even
for sentimental reasons. She wrote, "the tragedy is that we lost our mother
at the same time she lost what she had cherished the most, but your son's
encyclopedia."

Were I to believe in fate, I could say that when my grandmother heard
about our return "vacation," she did all she could to stay alive and see us
before her end. That could be true. I wish it were. But, the fact remains
that when we were in Cuba, she was in great physical pain unable to stay
awake for more than fifteen minutes at a time. My mother said she resembled a little girl. She was also almost blind, too. What were her dreams?
What were her fears? She never told me. She took them to her grave. I
often dream about my grandparents waiting for me after school: my
grandmother with a glass of *café con leche*; my grandfather ready for
another lesson in geography. I see them like that, their images flashing

effortlessly into my mind, and at those moments, I'm a kid again. Immortal.

My mother still seems to be at a loss when she speaks of Cuba. The first few days after coming back, she was very depressed. She would walk around the house as if lost, scrutinizing old pictures she'd been able to smuggle out of Cuba throughout the years. I had never seen her so down. She brooded a lot and there were times I'd find her late at night in front of the TV set watching my home video. As for my aunt, she went back to Puerto Rico with her family. She doesn't intend to go back to Cuba again, and short of a miracle, she probably intends to die in her adopted country, like so many Cubans.

Will I ever return to Cuba? That's a difficult answer. Cuba is a complex issue I can't understand with any satisfaction. And yet, despite my feelings, I hope that one day other Cuban-Americans feel the same curiosity I felt to rediscover what seems to be lost. Go and visit an uncle. An aunt. A grandmother. Honor your past. Crack that barrier that exists. Rediscover yourself. The Cuba of tomorrow belongs to all of us.

Let Cuba be reclaimed by this generation

By Jorge Reyes. Published Sunday, August 26, 2001 in <u>The Miami Herald</u>

I have been thinking a lot lately about the U.S. embargo and its ability, real or perceived, ultimately to bring about a democratically elected government in Cuba. In my most recent book, a personal memoir that included a visit to Cuba, I hardly touched on the subject. At the time I was writing it I didn't think politics was as important as the personal drama I sought to analyze.

However, since then, many things have occurred that have brought the entire dialogue of Cuba to the forefront (yes, I'm thinking of the Elián soap opera), causing me to change my own personal opinions. Prior to that time, my thoughts were not unlike what the vast majority of Cubans in exile think: With an embargo, Fidel will be history.

I left Cuba when I was 8 years old. Up until my visit, I thought very little of my country. I was too taken by my new adopted nation —by everything it gave me, by all the opportunities I had. Cuba, to my way of knowing, was a backward nation with a repressive form of government that stifled aspirations, hope and even happiness. The few times I thought about Cuba, I only thought about the bad things: having my hair forcefully trimmed at my elementary school; actos de repudios —acts of repudiation; the hardships; the hunger.

Why, I thought to myself, would anyone want to go back and visit?

As I grew older, my ideas matured, and my memories became laced with childhood nostalgia. It was Ernest Hemingway who said that memory is hunger. I often heard about the old house in the town in Boniato near the city of Santiago de Cuba. I often heard about my grandmother, now old, with cottony white hair and a face full of wrinkles, who every afternoon sat in the corridor of the house dressed in white cotton petticoats she still made by hand. She often asked any visitors from Miami about me, about my mother, about her other family members whom she hadn't seen in more than 20, then 30 years.

These thoughts, plus the terminal illness that finally consumed my grandmother, prompted me finally to ask my mother and an aunt to go back. They —especially my mother —had trepidations about going to Cuba. What were they going to find? What were they expecting to find?

We left Miami on a Friday afternoon and arrived in Boniato at the crack of dawn on Saturday. It took us almost 12 hours to arrive in a country that's only 45 minutes away. By the time we got to our hometown, the three of us were already tired, seeing our country as if in a dream. Cars, buses and horse-drawn carriages made up the traffic of Santiago at that hour.

The people seemed to live under circumstances that were, well, less than favorable. Homes had electricity, but blackouts underscored the strange realities of the peoples' existence. When there was light, it was so faint that everything took on a surreal pale glow that was nothing less than creepy.

Buses were filled to capacity, and the people on the buses usually hung from doors and windows, clinging desperately to each other by the hem of shirts or pants, whatever.

I devoted a very brief chapter to politics in my book. As I said, politics wasn't as important to me as the personal drama I sought to rediscover. And yet the tragedy of the Cuban people as a whole and Cuba's experiment in communism, or Fidelism, cannot be separated —complex as it may be, sad as it is —from political undertones.

It was then, on my trip to back, seeing this disaster all about me, that my ideas about Cuba began to change, and quick. The U.S. embargo hurts the people, not those in power. If the ultimate purpose of the embargo is to defeat Fidel by isolating him economically, socially and politically, it has failed in both rhetoric and in practice. Fidel, 42 years after his revolution, is still there, old and doddering, but still there nonetheless.

This, to me, is reason to enough to scrap this relic of the Cold War and come up with something better—and this should be done not because of Cuban politics but in spite of Fidelism and in spite, even, of the ire this view draws among many well-intentioned Cuban Americans in Miami. Further isolation makes no sense when the time is ripe to bombard Cuba with commerce, information and an influx of new ideas.

I often heard about my grandmother, now old, with cottony white hair and a face full of wrinkles.

All those who with Janus-like face only can look at an either-or situation miss the complexities of the Cuban nation and the countless, slow ways it will eventually turn into a pluralistic, multi-party political system.

I may be naive about my opinions. What I do know, though, is that there is a lot of work to be done in a post-Castro Cuba. The realities of that future demand new, fresh, imaginative ways to bring about a peaceful reconciliation among Cubans.

I don't have all the answers. What I do have is an open mind. Now is the time, more than ever, to breach this gap and cross that 90-mile stretch that to some of us is as wide as the universe. So I wrote in the book: "Go and visit an uncle. An aunt. A grandmother. Honor your past. Crack that barrier that exists. Rediscover yourself. The Cuba of tomorrow belongs to all of us."

My parents lost Cuba once. Don't let it happen again with this generation.

Descubriendo a Cuba

Esta es una carta a todo el pueblo de Cuba, dentro y fuera de la isla. Esta es una carta para los jovenes, para los viejos. Soy un joven Cubano-Americano que recientemente visitó a Cuba y escribí un libro basado en mis experiencias titulado, **Rediscovering Cuba: A Personal Memoir**, o **Redescubriendo Cuba: Memorias Personales**, en Español.

Salí de Cuba cuando tenia ocho años, hoy tengo veinte nueve. Antes de mi viaje a Cuba, no pensé mucho en lo que dejé en ella. Estaba enamorado con mi pais adoptivo—por todo lo que me daba, por todas las oportunidades que existen. Las pocas veces que pensaba en Cuba solo me acordaba de las cosas malas: tener mi pelo cortado forzosamente en mi escuela Antonio Roberts; los actos de repudios que mis padres tenian que aguantar; la miseria; el odio; la división; la opresión.

¿Porque? me preguntaba ¿quisiera regresar?

Segun fui creciendo, mis ideas maduraron y mis memorias se llenaron de nostalgia de mi niñez. De vez en cuando teníamos noticias de mi vieja casa en el pueblo de Boniato, cerca de la ciudad de Santiago. Me enteraba de chismes familiares, de mi abuela, ya una anciana, con su pelo mucho mas blanco, su cara repleta de arrugas, quien todas las tardes se sentaba en el portal de la casa y si algún visitante de Miami pasaba por Boniato, siempre le preguntaba por nosotros en Miami: por mi mamá, por mi papá, por mi.

Esa curiosidad, ese afán de conocer mis raíces, fueron las razones que me decidieron a regresar a un país que para mi es desconocido: para conocer aquéllos que habia dejado, para reconocer el amor que sentí por personas simples, buenas y llenos de amor campestre.

Mi mamá, una tía y yo salimos de Miami por la tarde, un Viernes, y llegamos al día siguiente a Boniato a las tres de la madrugada—doce horas de viajes a un país tan solo a 90 millas de las costas Americanas! Al llegar, llenó el ambiente un sentido surreal. Las calles estaban viejas, los carros tan antiguos como los edificios ya con mas de 40 años de continuo abandono. Las 'guaguas' o buses estaban llenas con personas agarrándose unos a los otros, de las puertas, de las ventanas. Cuando no habia otro medio de transportación, las carretillas se convertian en el vehículo popular. Pasé por el Cuartél Moncada, simbolo de la revolución, y todo estaba oscuro, nostalgico, en silencio aunque habia un carnavál.

Y al fin, despues de tanto, llegamos a Boniato, cansados, los ojos que se nos cerraban. Pero, estabamos aqui, despues de 20 años de ausencia.

Mirando a éste mundo mágico, atrapado en un pasado socialista, noté la desesperación de un pueblo deseando cambios fundamentales—aunque el tema de la politica se habla en susurros, el miedo es mucho. Mi pregunta ayer y hoy sigue siendo la misma: ¿Que va a pasar cuando Fidel se muera? ¿Qué o quien llenará el vacío politico y 'moral' en un pais donde no ha habido pluralidad de ideas por varias generaciones?

El mi libro casi no hablo de política. Pero, pensandolo bien, nosotros los Cubanos que vivimos fuera de Cuba, en el exilio, cometemos un gran delito si no rompemos las barreras que existen hoy entre los Cubanos en la isla. No importa que Fidel aun vive, que el *Fidelismo* se haya usado para perpetuar la separación de la nación Cubana. Para mi, todo eso es historia y solamente una curiosidad—el futuro es lo que me importa, no el odio y la desconfianza que comenzó el 31 de Diciembre de 1959. Mi generación de Cubanos-Americanos tiene que sobrepasar el pasado y ayudar a recrear un país exuberante, lleno de vida. Las realidades de ese futuro demanda nuevas, frescas e imaginativas ideas que vayan mas allá de las viejas polemicas del embargo, de la separación, del comunismo. Lo que Cuba necesita es un libre rejuego de ideas, no aislamiento; lo que Cuba necesita es un intercambio de ideas informales al pueblo fuera del contexto politico.

Se que no tengo todas las respuestas, lo que si tengo es una mente abierta.

Un mes después de mi visita, mi abuela falleció. Hoy, más que ayer, me siento feliz que la pude ver antes de su sueño eterno. Su amor, espera y curiosidad por nosotros en Miami, fueron ansias más grandes, mas poderosas, que ninguna ideología política que nos hubiese separado.

Mis padres perdieron a Cuba una vez. No dejen que suceda de nuevo. Como escribí en mi libro: "Visita un tio. Una tia. Una abuela. Rompe el hielo que existe. Redescubre lo que parece estar perdido," y llévele el mensaje de que existe otro mundo adonde la gente vive, trabaja, disfruta, discrepa pero adonde hay oportunidades para todos y sobre todo la libertad, sagrado derecho de todo ser humano.

An Interview with Jorge Reyes

Q: Which do you consider more important in your writing, a sense of place, your experiences, or something else altogether? Why is this important to you?
I can only write about what I know, the world that surrounds me and what I've been able to absorb from it. As a Cuban-American most of my writing, I think, reflects a sense of displacement, not belonging anywhere exactly. What's amazing to me is that we, Cubans, have been able to assimilate so well to the American ethos and at the same time hold on to so much of that world which is only 90 miles away from us, Cuba. It is this aspiration, this yearning and longing that I bring, or try to convey as best as I can, in my writing.

Q: Is there a particular aspect of your book (or books) that you are most proud of?
I am proud of the book simply because I finished it. I never, ever, thought of writing something as personal unless I thought I had something to share with the world, not just the Cuban community. I wanted my experiences to be appealing so that anyone can read about them and enjoy the book for what it is—a highly personal conversation with myself about a universal theme: rediscovering one's roots. Also, I wanted non-Cubans to understand why we, Cubans living as exiles, feel the way we do about our homeland. In the wake of the Elian Gonzalez fiasco, many outside of this community saw us as oddballs.

Q: Now that you brought it up, what do you think of the Elian case?
Elian, unfortunately, became the poster boy of a cause when he shouldn't
have. After all, how can anyone disagree to have a little boy reunited with
his dad? However, keep in mind, though, that after I returned from Cuba,
I don't see the 1959 Cuban Revolution the same way: there is nothing
romantic about it, nor should it be admired. The same Cuban government that wanted to reunite father and son is the same government that
for over forty years has been systematically dividing families, my own
included! Why couldn't we, the exiled Cubans, have said this more
emphatically? But, I guess one has to live through this repressive machin-
ery in order to understand how brutal it truly is and why we oppose it so
much. If we were not successful articulating this then, we must start doing
it. The time is ripe. But I'm veering away from the subject, this book is not
about politics.

**Q: What is unique about your book, what differentiates it from other
books in the same category? What about it will reach out and grab the
reader?**
Unlike many books, I wrote this book while I was in Cuba, in seven days.
It reads like a diary because it is a diary. Many of the mistakes in diaries are
found in the book! In a single sentence, I would write about something
that happened during the day and on the next sentence about the carnival
at night. Also, I wrote it in a "slangy" "Spanglish" way because that's
exactly who I am and how I express myself—well, now that I think about
it, probably half of Miami speaks this way, too. On a more personal note,
I tend to think of myself as young, therefore what I wrote were only observations from anecdotes, hearsays and gossip. I didn't spend years research-
ing what I wrote about. Also, unlike the majority of books on Cuba, I
wasn't embittered about the whole division of the Cuban nation as most of
my ancestors are. I don't feel it in me. To me, all that is history. The future
is what interests me.

Q: What are your influences and inspirations? What makes you write?
I don't know what makes me write. The creative process is a mystery. Were I to be Irish, German, whatever, I think I would still write. I guess this is therapy. As far influences, there isn't one writer I've been influenced by—there have been many. But, I couldn't point them out to you. Maybe you can. I don't know. I would like to think that I have my own voice. Interestingly enough, many people who have read this book have mentioned that it reads more like fiction. It isn't. Some even mention the dream-like quality and compare it to Marquez, Cortazar, et al.

Q: Are you working on something now? In what ways is it a departure from what you've done in the past?
Not a departure, really. I'm always working on simultaneous things. I'm now finishing a book of poetry. After that I want to put the finishing touches on a collection of short stories, and after—way after—take out a draft of a novel that has been gathering dust in my cabinet for many years.

About the author

Jorge Reyes, a long-time resident of South Florida, was born in Santiago de Cuba. He graduated cum laude from Barry University in Miami with a Bachelor's degree in political science and history. He has previously published short stories, articles and poetry in various magazines and newspapers such as the Miami Herald, Generation ñ, Gablers Magazine, the Torch.

0-595-19457-5

Printed in the United States
83671LV00005B/472-486/A